auals

Modern
SHORT PLAYS

Selected and Edited

by

FELIX SPER, Ph.D.

THOMAS JEFFERSON HIGH SCHOOL
BROOKLYN, NEW YORK

GLOBE BOOK COMPANY • **NEW YORK**

Copyright, 1952

by

Globe Book Company, Inc.

INTRODUCTION

THE SHORT PLAY

What the short story is to the novel, the short play is to the full-length play in three or more acts. The form may be compared to a miniature in painting, to a cameo, or to a statuette. The outlines of a long play simply shrink to a single situation or character within a narrow frame. In plain theatre talk, any play that unwinds a story or plot within a period of from fifteen minutes (the French *quart d'heure*) to forty minutes may be called a one-act play or playlet.

As a type the short play has come down from a number of older forms. In the last two centuries it was customary for theatres to lengthen an evening's entertainment by adding to the main play a short comedy or farce called the *afterpiece*. After 1880 dramatic acts in humorous or sentimental dialogue were acted out as features in music halls and later in vaudeville shows.

A queer offshoot appeared in Paris over seventy years ago in the shortplay theatre called Le Grand Guignol. Here sensational farces and thrillers chilled the spines of the audience. Dissatisfied writers studied these theatrical effects but built them around more serious ideas with real characters in everyday circumstances. Since then the phrase "slice of life" has been applied to the dramatization of actual situations with real persons acting out their problems against settings with real doors and real walls. Everyday problems, no matter how ugly or mean, became the subject of many one-acters. Because such plays tried to copy nature faithfully, they became known as *naturalistic*.

Out of the need to quiet restless early-comers to the theatre

and to whet their appetites for the main dish to follow came
the practice of showing a long one-act play known as a
"curtain-raiser." Most celebrated of this class was *Box and
Cox* by James Morton, which ran the circuits of England for
years during the middle of the previous century.

The modern one-act play in the United States dates from
an important theatrical invasion. In 1911 the Irish Players of
Dublin came to this country. Thereafter a fresh wind started
blowing through the theatre. Especially the folk-plays of
J. M. Synge created an interest in folk characters and regional
themes. Plays in imitation written soon afterward inspired
the writing of vital one-act pieces for our stage.

In revolt against the professional theatre, hundreds of
amateur theatres sprang up on the wave of a little theatre
movement. Among the new playhouses were The Washington Square Players—later to become the Theatre Guild—the
Neighborhood Playhouse, The Provincetown Playhouse
(transferred from Cape Cod to Manhattan) which gave
Eugene O'Neill his first chance to write his sea-sketches.
Responding to the new theatrical currents, players from
Madison, Boston, Chicago, and groups from experimental
laboratories in universities everywhere from Chapel Hill,
North Carolina to Seattle, Washington stirred new audiences
across the country. In addition, women's clubs, high school
casts, churches, and labor unions felt the urge to act out
short plays domestic and foreign, folk and sophisticated. At
its peak the one-act play ranged from fantasy to hard-boiled
realism; from dainty cream-puffs to strong meat.

In the thirties a powerful sentiment in favor of themes on
industrial problems held the boards and gave strength to the
new type. Of late years the supply of one-act plays has swung
between school plays on conventional adolescent subjects for
high schools and the fewer plays on solid themes developed
by characters who rule the plot. Typical of the second variety

are such well-written dramas as *Hymn to the Rising* Sun by Paul Green, *The Happy Journey* by Thornton Wilder, and *Hope is The Thing With Feathers* by Richard Harrity.

In England the short dramatic sketch, long admired and enjoyed, continues to entertain crowds in the provincial theatre. Occasionally along with broadly comic scenes and odd characters have been shown more sober studies like *The Monkey's Paw, Lonesome-Like, The Will,* and *Children of Darkness.*

British theatres have been competing in British play festivals for many years and therefore have been demanding well-written, effective, original playlets, while the classic pieces by Pinero, Barrie, Shaw, and lesser names have been used conservatively by the top theatres in large cities.

Today the United States is studded with small, non-professional playhouses where thousands of enthusiastic companies, often aided by professional directors and actors, enjoy putting on plays and sometimes short plays preferably original. If such are not available, directors turn to Broadway hits.

Naturally the professional theatre remains the mainstay of the drama. Of late years scores of theatres outside Broadway, both rural and municipal, have made their appearance. These continue to operate under such varied names as little, community, civic, campus, church, labor-union, and arena theatres. Though aims may differ, basically they all crave an outlet for creative energies directed toward designing settings, directing, acting, and sometimes writing plays of many varieties.

The radio market has absorbed large numbers of playlets together with a shortened version of Broadway play to be acted within one hour's time. Typical of the superior species that have been broadcast over major networks are the two radio plays included in this volume. The technique is still that of the one-act play but with one difference: its appeal is to the ear. By stressing the sharp, concrete word spoken with sound effects and incidental music, the impact on the mind of the listener is multiplied. Likewise the reader can readily call up vivid mental pictures and create the sequences in his own imagination. Television too has revived the vaudeville sketch and the skit, and now and then uses short comedies and tragedies.

The one-act plays here presented derive from outside countries like Hungary, Spain, and Great Britain as well as from the United States of America. Though settings may differ, themes are rooted in common experiences of young and old. One excerpt from a long play of the kind known as episodic has been included because it satisfies the demands of unity and separateness.

Finally this collection aims to capture a medley of moods both tender and tough, comic and pathetic. Sometimes the shadow of one falls upon the other as in life, and the result is a blend of laughter and tears. Deep or light as the treatment may be, the product cannot fail to offer insights into character along with amusement. We smile thoughtfully or shake our heads as we recognize situations which might have happened to us. In short, we have visited regions somewhat different from our own, seen a strip of life, and therefore feel better and wiser for the knowledge gained.

Let us now rummage among the scripts on the green-room shelf and pull out a dozen and more for the benefit of the playreader who, unable to go to the theatre, can still bring to life the scenes and characters on the stage of his own creating.

THE FRAMEWORK   *the event*

To understand the one-act play one should, after reading, try to analyze the series of incidents known as the plot. Like any mechanism, it can be taken apart and examined. The same elements as used in the long play will be found shortened and contracted, with everything in excess severely cut.

The single plot moves according to this line:

Exposition: a quick introduction of characters and the problem. Who's who and what's what.

Complication: tying the incidents or events together without delay until a knot is tied; the plot begins to spin.

Crisis: the highest point of suspense in which the characters have to make a decision; the peak of the action.

Resolution: the answer to the crisis; the compromise or solution; the knot is now unwound.

In brief, any play, short or long, which dramatizes a situation honestly and truthfully must follow the logic of cause and effect, and thereby show that motives follow the law of probability. Characters must act naturally as they would within the given framework of events. Dialogue should sound as natural as the language one hears on the street or in the home. Let it be understood that poetry can definitely heighten the power of speech and make it sound impressive and agreeable to the ear.

For helpful suggestions offered, I express thanks to Dr. Joseph Mersand of Long Island City High School, to Mrs. Anne L. Harris and Miss Carrie Dulakis, both of Thomas Jefferson High School, and to Dr. Lawrence H. Feigenbaum of Eastern District High School, for valuable counsel.

F.S.

CONTENTS

TWO SLAPS IN THE FACE

Juvenile Dialogue

by

FERENC MOLNAR

This funny trifle on the school-boy level illustrates Molnar's keen observation of town youngsters.

Molnar's expert technique and clever dialogue have made his dozen plays popular throughout the world. He is the author of the well-known "Liliom" which was transformed years later into the successful musical play, *Carousel.*

FERENC MOLNAR
Popular Hungarian dramatist.

TWO SLAPS IN THE FACE

CHARACTERS

JULES, *a youth*

ALFRED, *a youth*

A Budapest street at two o'clock of a sunny autumn afternoon.

JULES *and* ALFRED *are walking home from school, carrying their books under their arms. Neither is quite seventeen.*

JULES. You haven't said a word for ten minutes.

ALFRED. No.

JULES. Don't you feel well?

ALFRED. I'm all right.

JULES. You have been depressed all day.

ALFRED. Yes. . . . I'm depressed.

JULES. Why?

ALFRED. Because women are so deceitful.
  [*There is a pause*]

JULES. You mean Vilma?

ALFRED. Of course. . . . Vilma. Who else?
  [*Another pause*]

JULES. What has she done?

ALFRED. She hasn't done anything special. She is deceitful, that's all. Women are all alike.

JULES. What happened, anyhow?

ALFRED. You know that water tower on Marguerite Island?

JULES. Yes.

ALFRED. Lots of fellows and girls meet there in the evening. She and I used to meet there too.

3

JULES. At the water tower?

ALFRED. Yes. At six every afternoon. She'd say she had a music lesson, and I'd say I was going to the library, and we'd meet at the tower and go walking under the trees as all lovers do . . . only ours was an innocent affair, for I never even kissed her because she was afraid someone might see us. No, I'd only take her arm, and we'd walk along and talk about the future . . . when we'd be married, and things like that. And sometimes we'd quarrel about her music teacher. I was a little jealous of him. I tried to make Vilma jealous, too, but she'd never show her jealousy. She's too clever. But she loves me——

JULES. Yes, but what happened?

ALFRED. I'm coming to that. . . . So we always met at the water tower until one day her mother intercepted a letter. . . . It was my own fault. I didn't have to write a letter at all, much less put the water tower in it. I could have written "the usual place," but, like a fool, I wrote "the water tower." . . . Well, her mother intercepted the letter but never said a word to Vilma about it. And the next afternoon she watches Vilma tying a new hair ribbon in a double bow, and when Vilma says "Music lesson" she pretends to believe her and lets her go without a word. But she follows her. You see?

JULES. Oh!

ALFRED. It was terrible. There I stood in front of the tower, never suspecting a thing. And Vilma came up. "Hello!" "Hello!" we said to each other, and arm in arm we walked toward the trees. I asked her if she loved me, and she said of course she did. I asked her if she loved me very much, and she said very much. I said, "I adore you." And she said, "Not as much as I adore you." I said: "It is impossible for anyone to be adored as much as I adore you." And at that ment her mother rushes up like a bull.

JULES. How do you mean—like a bull?

ALFRED. Like a female bull. She rushed up and planted herself in front of us. I felt like running away, but I couldn't leave Vilma alone in trouble. . . . She just stood there glaring at both of us. She never said a word to me. She couldn't; she doesn't know me. But she grabbed hold of Vilma, and shrieked: "So this is your music lesson! So this is why you put a new ribbon in your hair!" Poor Vilma couldn't say a word. She only stood there, trembling. Then suddenly that wild bull of a mother raised her hand, and, before I could prevent it, she gave Vilma a slap in the face . . . an awful slap in the face.

JULES. In the face?

ALFRED. Right in the face! And before I could say a word she had grabbed Vilma by the hand and led her away. There I stood looking after them. I can't explain to you how badly I felt. But I loved Vilma more than ever, because I knew how humiliated she must feel, having her face slapped like that in my presence. So I went home.

JULES. Is that all?

ALFRED. No. The worst is yet to come. Next day I wrote to Vilma, asking her to meet me at the tower on Thursday. I reasoned it would be safer than ever now, because after what had happened, her mother would never suppose she'd meet me again.

JULES. Did she come?

ALFRED. Certainly she came. She cried as if her heart would break. I knew she'd be humiliated. She kept repeating over and over again: "If she only hadn't done it in front of you! If she had slapped me at home I wouldn't have minded half as much." Nothing I could say seemed to console

her. Vilma is an awfully proud girl. She didn't stay v
long. She had to go home. And as I was going home myseh,
an idea came to me.

JULES. What was that?

ALFRED. An idea of how to make it up to her for the slap
she got on my account.

JULES. How?

ALFRED. If I hadn't written that stupid letter her mother
would never have slapped her in my presence. Well, the only
way to make it up to her was to have my father slap me in
her presence. Do you see?

JULES. No.

ALFRED. Very simple. I wrote my father an anonymous
letter in a disguised hand. "Dear Sir, Every day at six your
son meets a girl at the water tower on Marguerite Island. If
you don't believe me, go there and watch for him, and box
the young scoundrel's ears as he deserves." Signed, "A
Friend."

JULES. Did you send it to him?

ALFRED. Certainly. That suggestion about boxing the
young scoundrel's ears wasn't strictly necessary. I know my
father pretty well; and I was almost certain that if he caught
me, he'd hit me of his own accord. But I had to make absolutely sure, so as to be even with Vilma. She gets one from
her mother as a lady; I get one from my father as a gentleman; then there is no reason for her to feel humiliated any
longer. Wasn't that the chivalrous thing to do?

JULES. Absolutely.

ALFRED. A gentleman could do no less.

JULES. No.

ALFRED. I sent the letter, and I could see in father's face
that he got it all right. He kept his eye on me all afternoon,

and at quarter to six, when I was going out, he asked me where. I said: "To the library." And, sure enough, when I left the house he followed me, keeping about a block behind on the other side of the street. I was pleased. I reach the tower and I wait. Father came up on the other side and hid himself among the trees. I pretended not to see him. In about five minutes Vilma came. "Hello! Hello!" we said to each other. "How are you? . . . Do you love me? . . . I love you." . . . I took her arm and led her toward the trees. And when we get there the old man pounces down on me. "Library, eh? You young scamp!" He gives me a choice line of language and before he had finished—exactly as I had planned it—he gives me a nice ringing slap on the face with his open hand. "Come along now!" he roars, and leads me away. But as we went he raised his hat politely to Vilma. It was a courteous act. I respect him for it.

JULES. Yes, it was.

ALFRED. The next day I meet Vilma again. What do you suppose she does? She laughs at me.

JULES. Laughs?

ALFRED. Laughs! . . . She said the expression on my face when father slapped me was the most comical thing she had ever seen. And she began laughing all over again. . . . Then I told her how I had planned the whole thing myself. I showed her a copy of the letter, and explained how I had humiliated myself to make it up to her for her own humiliation, and that it was nothing to laugh about; but she only went on laughing and laughing like a silly fool. And when I reproached her she said: "I can't help it. Since I saw your father slap you I can't respect you any more."

JULES. Is that what she said?

ALFRED. Would you believe it? . . . Yes. . . . I felt my face getting redder and redder. I couldn't say another word.

And when she saw how humiliated I was, she became a bit
sorry for me. "If you knew how ridiculous you looked when
he slapped you," she explained. "It's no use for me to try
ever to love you again. I couldn't. I'm quite disillusioned."
Then she started giggling all over again, and I walked away.
I can still hear her laughing.

JULES. And now it's all over?

ALFRED. All over.

[*There is a pause.*]

JULES. She's not worth grieving about. She's fickle.

ALFRED. They're all like that. . . . What's the use of being
chivalrous? You let yourself be slapped in the face for them,
and they only laugh at you.

JULES. You'd think she'd love you all the more after a
sacrifice like that.

ALFRED. Yes, that's the baffling part of it. After her wild
mother slapped her I loved her more than ever before . . .
and respected her more, too. But she—she—— It's so unreasonable! I don't understand it at all.

JULES. Neither do I.

[*They walk on, shaking their heads dolefully.*]

CURTAIN

PROLOGUE TO GLORY

Historic Episode

ACT TWO—SCENE THREE

E. P. CONKLE

Ellsworth Prouty Conkle's interest in folk characters has found expression in a number of plays, long and short. With tender humor and homely wisdom he here pictures young Lincoln in and about New Salem, Illinois. In this scene, we see Lincoln facing one of the most shocking events in his life: the death of his beloved.

The play from which this scene is taken, "Prologue to Glory" was originally produced by the Federal Theatre in 1936.

Dr. E. P. Conkle is a professor of English at the University of Texas.

"Prologue to Glory," act II scene III—Interior scene

PROLOGUE TO GLORY

CHARACTERS

ABE LINCOLN

MRS. RUTLEDGE

STRANGER

COLONEL RUTLEDGE

GRANNY

DOCTOR

Interior of Rutledge Inn.

A log-cabin room; a fireplace with a low fire; table and chairs; bracket lamps; doors to outside, bedroom, kitchen. Outdoors—a soughing wind.

Discovered: GRANNY RUTLEDGE *in rocker, rocking, reading Bible, footstool at her feet.* COLONEL RUTLEDGE *on bench, head in hand.* ABE *stands near window.* A STRANGER *near the fire-place.* MRS. RUTLEDGE *enters from bedroom with lighted candle; goes to kitchen.*

ABE. How is Ann?

MRS. RUTLEDGE. She's sleeping now.

ABE. Yes?

[MRS. RUTLEDGE *goes into kitchen.* ABE *stands looking after her.*]

STRANGER. Sorry your dorter's under the weather, Colonel.

COLONEL. Milk-sick.[1]

STRANGER. Ummm! Call it the trembles where I come

---

[1] A disease caused by eating milk or butter or flesh of cattle poisoned by certain plants.

11

from. [ABE *turns, looks through window.*] S'pose you've tried bark, and jalap, and boneset tea?

COLONEL. We've tried everything—everything.

[*Silence. The* STRANGER *turns to* GRANNY.]

STRANGER. You're readin' a mighty fine book thur, Granny.

GRANNY. No finer ever writ, Stranger.

STRANGER. We grow in love—and arrive at grace aboundin'.

GRANNY. Amen.

[*Silence.*]

STRANGER. [*To* ABE.] Say, young feller, you must have plenty of gumption to run ag'in old Pete Cartwright.

ABE. Yeh.

STRANGER. How d'you stand on th' slavery question, Linkern?

ABE. I ain't been thinkin' much about slavery lately, Stranger. [*He sits.*]

STRANGER. Well, no. But you air a politician, ain't you? These yur Abolitionists says the slaves ort to be set free. Then the—

ABE. I reckon no one's got more sympathy for the sore-oppressed than me. But we can't afford to make up our minds till we know the facts. Southerners would stand to lose millions if they were freed. Seems to me whether slavery is or is not wrong depends on whether the slave is or is not a *man.* I think—I—don't rightly keer to talk of it now, Stranger. [*He turns away, looking down.*]

STRANGER. [*Looking toward bedroom.*] Your sweetheart, mebby?

ABE. Ye-e-es—

STRANGER. [*Turns toward* COLONEL; *takes watch from pocket and looks at it.*] Eight-thirty! Hi-de-hum! well—Good night, Colonel. Good night, Granny.

COLONEL. Good night. Good sleep.

[STRANGER *goes through kitchen door.*]

STRANGER. [*Outside.*] Good night, Mrs. Rutledge.

MRS. RUTLEDGE. Good night. [*She enters; goes to* COLO-NEL.] Doc hasn't come yet?

COLONEL. [*Standing.*] No. He's probably not back from Decatur yet.

[ABE *gets up.*]

MRS. RUTLEDGE. What if they don't have any calomel[1] over there, John?

COLONEL. They're sure to have it at Renshaw's.

MRS. RUTLEDGE. [*Turning to* ABE.] I've got your supper set out, Abe. Can't you go in and try to eat a bite?

ABE. I ain't much hungry.

MRS. RUTLEDGE. We must keep our own strength, Abe. [ABE *turns away.*] Come, Father, I think you should close the shutter tight.

[*Both go into bedroom.*]

ABE. [*Paces up and down; stops by footstool.*] Granny—

GRANNY. Yes, Abe?

ABE. Do you 'spect the calomel will help her?

GRANNY. [*Rocking.*] Maybe. Maybe only the dear Jesus cain do that now, Abe.

ABE. But she seemed better this afternoon, Granny! [*Sitting on stool.*] She even wanted me to tell her a story and—it can't be that—it—why she was even sitting up in bed, Granny! And I told her the story about little Bud and she laughed and—

GRANNY. [*Rocking.*] It lingers—lingers. She's a brave little

[1] A strong, purgative drug.

soldier, Abe, but she's mighty bad sick. You might as well know that. I've laid five of my own away with th' trembles. They was all—bright leetle critters!

ABE. If we could *do* something!

GRANNY. Maybe you'd better'd get a mite of sleep. I kin set up. I kin watch.

ABE. [*Bending head into hands.*] I can't sleep. I can't eat. I can't do nothin' but—

GRANNY. [*Rocking.*] She loved th' spicewood fire. I've seen her set here by it for hours—her leetle pinafore—singin' and mendin'—

ABE. [*Looking up.*] They cain't carry her off now—in her young years—when she's just beginnin' to live.

GRANNY. [*Rocking.*] They tuk leetle Robby—

ABE. We'd only begun to know our love—to plan things out in the years—to realize! And—now . . . this! All—going! Going!

GRANNY. [*Rocking.*] They tuk leetle Mercy—

ABE. Waiting! Helpless and waiting! If a man could only rise up and do something!

GRANNY. [*Rocking.*] Sech bright leetle critters!

ABE. I went through something like this once before! Someone you love—standing helpless—waiting. I set day by day reading Ma parts of the Bible she liked best. On the sixth day she called me to her bed—talked of many strange things— principalities and powers—and things present—and things to come—urged me and Sairy always to walk in paths of good- ness and truth—told us many things would come t'him that served God—an' th' best way t'—serve Him was to serve His people. [*Pause.*] She was amongst the lowliest of mankind. She walked the earth with her poor feet in the dust—her head in the stars—[*Pause.*] Pa took me down into the woods t'make her a coffin. Pa was sawin' and ı was hammerin' the pegs in. The hammer dropped at my feet; it was like someone was drivin' 'em into my heart. It's—just goin' through all that again—now!

GRANNY. Yes, Abry.

ABE. [*Getting up; agony.*] How much does the Lord require of a man? [*The* DOCTOR *enters carrying a pillcase.* ABE *goes to him.*] You got the calomel, Doc?

DOCTOR. Yes, Abe, I got it. How's she been?

ABE. Sleepin'. They're in there with her. Doc, you've got to do something—!

DOCTOR. I'll do all I can do! [*Goes to bedroom door.*] Evenin' Granny. [*He goes in; closes door.* ABE *looks after him.*]

GRANNY. [*Low.*] It's comin'—comin'— [ABE *turns sharply, looks at her.*] Abe, come throw on another log. It's gettin' cold in yur— [*She huddles up.* ABE *comes to fireplace, puts log on fire.*] —wind a-raisin'—raisin'—

[*The* DOCTOR *comes slowly out.* GRANNY *rocks.*]

ABE. [*Anxiously to* DOCTOR.] Doc—she's better? She's only a little—tired? She—?

DOCTOR. She's mighty tired, Abe.

ABE. [*To* DOCTOR.] She'll get well? She—?

DOCTOR. It's only a matter of minutes—Abe. She—was calling, Abe.

ABE. *Me—?*

DOCTOR. Yes.

[*The* DOCTOR *takes* ABE's *arm; leads him to bedroom door.* ABE *goes in, afraid, leaving door ajar.*]

GRANNY. [*Rocking.*] They tuk leetle Robby—they tuk leetle Mercy—

[*The sound of* MRS. RUTLEDGE, *crying. The* DOCTOR *crosses to the kitchen door.*]

DOCTOR. I'll just be out here—in the kitchen—Granny—
[*He leaves. Weeping in bedroom.*]

GRANNY. [*In prayer.*] Dear God, be with us in our hour of
need. Keep her precious unto Thee until we shall meet in
the Sweet Bye and Bye. [ABE *comes to the doorway.*] Sustain
us who are afflicted that we may be more as Thee in Thy
hour!

[*The* COLONEL *comes; puts a hand on* ABE's *shoulder.*]

COLONEL. I guess we've got to bear these things like men,
Abe!

ABE. [*Anguish.*] I've—I've got to *feel* it like a man, first!
[*He crosses to the outside door, rushes into the night.* GRANNY
rocks.]

CURTAIN

TOO MANY HANDS ON A WATCH

Light Comedy

by

WILLIAM H. MORGAN

In this quick-moving and amusing sketch built around the theme of the cheater cheated, we have a good example of clever workmanship in creating incident and character.

As no information on the author's identity could be obtained, the reader may invent a biography or let the playlet speak for itself.

WILLIAM H. MORGAN

TOO MANY HANDS ON A WATCH

CHARACTERS

MR. FOSSEL

MRS. FOSSEL

TILLIE

JOE KINNEY

MR. FOSSEL, *a young man of about 28. He is not very robust, and his pale face gives the impression of a man who has worked very hard to make good and has had very little play in his life.*

MRS. FOSSEL, *a slightly plump woman of about the same age, with a Mary Boland manner. She has a querulous, somewhat high-pitched voice, and a very bossy personality. Underneath her dominant exterior, however, is a very sentimental side.*

TILLIE, *wide-eyed, loquacious, and somewhat dull in mentality. She expresses everything she feels in speech and facial expression.*

JOE KINNEY, *a big, gruff, surly thug, who is well satisfied with himself. He appears in a turtle-necked sweater, and coat, and shows need of a shave. He wears a cap pulled down over one eye.*

SCENE. Living room at the Fossels. 6 P. M.

There is a center table with two drawers, downstage center, and a couch with back and sides to stage left of table, and a comfortable chair, large and roomy, to stage right of

*the two table drawers which are open. She continues to
search for several seconds, with a worried expression.*

MRS. FOSSEL. [*calls to stage right.*] Tillie.

TILLIE. [*answers from outside right.*] Yes, ma'am.

MRS. FOSSEL. Did you find it?

TILLIE. [*outside.*] No, ma'am. It's not here.

MRS. FOSSEL. Oh, dear, what will I do? [*She searches
through righthand drawer. Calls again.*] Come here a moment, will you, Tillie?

TILLIE. [*outside right.*] Yes, ma'am, I'm coming. [*Mrs.
Fossel continues to search. In a few seconds Tillie enters
from right.*] I looked everywhere, ma'am, but it ain't there.

MRS. FOSSEL. Oh, dear, I wouldn't have lost that watch for
the world. [*Walks to left.*]

TILLIE. Was it very valuable, ma'am?

MRS. FOSSEL. Yes, Tillie, it was. It had a Swiss movement,
and I forget how many jewels in it.

TILLIE. Oh, that's too bad.

MRS. FOSSEL. It wasn't just the watch itself that was
valuable, though I think it was ten-karat gold. It was the
associations that went with it.

TILLIE. I see.

MRS. FOSSEL. Mr. Fossel's Uncle Henry carried it through
the World War.

TILLIE. [*tries to show surprise.*] Is that so?

MRS. FOSSEL. Yes, and Uncle Henry's father carried it
through the Spanish-American War.

TILLIE. Think of it. That watch certainly saw service,
didn't it?

MRS. FOSSEL. It certainly did.

TILLIE. It's a wonder it kept going that long.

MRS. FOSSEL. Well, they wound it of course, and kept it repaired, and then too, I imagine, they didn't drop it often.

TILLIE. That must have been hard to do, in the war.

MRS. FOSSEL. Yes, I imagine it was, but that old watch still kept good time. Except for a cracked face, it still has a good appearance.

TILLIE. It certainly stood for a lot of handling, didn't it?

MRS. FOSSEL. [*looks up dreamily.*] It certainly did. [*Starts up.*] But, Tillie, we're forgetting it's gone. We must do something about it.

TILLIE. Yes, ma'am, I'll do whatever you say.

MRS. FOSSEL. [*walks up and down.*] Oh, Mr. Fossel will be so annoyed when he hears it. He just loved that watch.

TILLIE. Must you tell him?

MRS. FOSSEL. Oh, Tillie, of course I must tell him. Uncle Henry gave him that on his twenty-first birthday.

TILLIE. I see, well I just thought as long as he never carried it, he might think *he* lost it.

MRS. FOSSEL. Oh, Tillie, it wouldn't be honest not to tell him. There's such a thing as conscience, you know.

TILLIE. I see. Well, of course I don't know much about those things.

MRS. FOSSEL. But can't you think of where it might be?

TILLIE. Where did you think you saw it last, Mrs. Fossel?

MRS. FOSSEL. [*she points to right-hand drawer.*] It was right in this drawer.

TILLIE. Are you sure?

MRS. FOSSEL. No, I remember now. I took it out and put it on the shelf in the kitchen.

MRS. FOSSEL. No, of course I wouldn't. I only put it there while I talked to the milkman.

TILLIE. Maybe he took it.

MRS. FOSSEL. Don't interrupt, please. From the kitchen I took it upstairs and put it on my bureau. Yes, that's what I did with it. I put it on my bureau.

TILLIE. Well, it ain't there now. I looked.

MRS. FOSSEL. [*deep in thought.*] No, I know it isn't there now—because I put it there before I moved the bureau to the other side of the room, and that was last Wednesday— or was it Tuesday?

TILLIE. It was Tuesday, ma'am, for that was the day we cleaned the room.

MRS. FOSSEL. Yes, that's right, it was Tuesday. It's funny, Tillie, that you never saw it.

TILLIE. Oh, I've seen it many times, but I didn't see it Tuesday. That's the one day I didn't see it, and I haven't seen it since.

MRS. FOSSEL. All right, Tillie, drop it, but what could have happened to the watch is more than I can see.

TILLIE. Maybe somebody took it.

MRS. FOSSEL. Yes, I thought of that, too, but there hasn't been anyone here but you and I, and I know I didn't take it.

TILLIE. And you know I didn't take it, don't you, Mrs. Fossel?

MRS. FOSSEL. Well, of course, Tillie, if you didn't see it, I suppose you couldn't have taken it.

TILLIE. No, ma'am. That proves I didn't.

MRS. FOSSEL. [*looks suspiciously at Tillie.*] Well, it's mighty funny what happened to it.

TILLIE. Maybe the plumber took it. He was here last Tuesday, fixing that bathroom spigot.

MRS. FOSSEL. That's right, he was . . . [*Hesitates.*] And he's just the one who took it.

TILLIE. But, of course, ma'am, maybe he didn't.

MRS. FOSSEL. I'm afraid there's no maybe to it. I never did trust that man, and I wouldn't have had him, except that he's the only plumber near.

TILLIE. I noticed he had a watch of his own, ma'am.

MRS. FOSSEL. Yes, I don't doubt he has many watches of his own. Ours became his own, last Tuesday.

TILLIE. What makes you think he took it, Mrs. Fossel?

MRS. FOSSEL. He has gray eyes, Tillie, and I don't trust people with gray eyes.

TILLIE. My father had gray eyes.

MRS. FOSSEL. I'm sorry, Tillie. I don't suppose your father could help it, but we knew a man with gray eyes once, who stole a whole business from Mr. Fossel.

TILLIE. Couldn't he stop him?

MRS. FOSSEL. No, he couldn't. He opened up a store, right opposite to Mr. Fossel's, and in a year he had taken all the business.

TILLIE. Did he do it with his eyes?

MRS. FOSSEL. Don't be silly, Tillie. He didn't do it with his eyes, but only a man with *his* eyes could have done it.

TILLIE. Oh, I see what you mean, now.

MRS. FOSSEL. I've never liked gray eyes since.

TILLIE. I see. Are you going to tell Mr. Fossel that the plumber took his watch?

MRS. FOSSEL. I certainly am.

TILLIE. Oh, I wouldn't if I was you. Did you see him bend that pipe with his b———

MRS. FOSSEL. Mr. Fossel can look after him.

TILLIE. Who's to look after Mr. Fossel?

MRS. FOSSEL. That will do, Tillie, please.

[*A door closes outside at right.*]

TILLIE. Here comes Mr. Fossel now, ma'am.

MRS. FOSSEL. [*listens.*] Yes, that's he. Well, I'm glad he's here. I want to tell him, and get it over with.

[*She walks to door right.*]

MR. FOSSEL. [*enters from door right.*] Hello, dear. [*They embrace.*] I'm a little late, but don't have supper right away, if you don't mind. There's something I want to tell you.

MRS. FOSSEL. There's something I want to tell you, too.

MR. FOSSEL. It's nothing very important, is it?

MRS. FOSSEL. Yes, James, I'm afraid it is. Your watch has been stolen, by the plumber who was here last Tuesday.

MR. FOSSEL. Do you mean the watch Uncle Henry gave me?

MRS. FOSSEL. Yes, I'm sorry to say, and I'm to blame. I was careless with it, I'll admit.

MR. FOSSEL. But dear, you're not to blame at all. I took the watch.

MRS. FOSSEL. You took it?

MR. FOSSEL. Yes. I took it last Tuesday, to have the face fixed.

MRS. FOSSEL. Oh, dear, why didn't you tell me?

MR. FOSSEL. I forgot, dear. I saw it on your bureau, and I felt ashamed of myself for not having it fixed, so I stuck it in my pocket.

TILLIE. See, Mrs. Fossel, the plumber with the gray eyes didn't take it, after all.

MRS. FOSSEL. Hush, Tillie, please. I don't want to hear

any more about it. It's found, and that's all I care about.

MR. FOSSEL. But it isn't found, Mary, at least not yet. That's what I wanted to tell you. A pickpocket must have taken it out of my pocket, last Tuesday, on my way down town.

MRS. FOSSEL. How do you know it was taken?

MR. FOSSEL. Well, I advertised for it on Wednesday, in the Evening Times, saying no questions would be asked, and the crook who has it phoned me today.

TILLIE. [*laughs.*] Oh, my, doesn't that poor watch have adventures, though. Think of the people who had their hands on it—first your Uncle Henry, and his father, then you, then Mrs. Fossel, then me, then you again, then the crook, then maybe the jeweler. [*Laughs.*] The poor plumber never had a chance.

MRS. FOSSEL. That will do, Tillie, please.

MR. FOSSEL. Yes, Tillie, warm the supper, please. We won't eat 'till about seven-thirty. I expect a caller first.

TILLIE. Yes, sir.

MRS. FOSSEL. Who's coming?

MR. FOSSEL. I'll explain later, dear.

[*Tillie still stands listening.*]

MRS. FOSSEL. That will do, Tillie; you may go.

TILLIE. Yes, ma'am.

[*She exits left.*]

MRS. FOSSEL. [*turns to Mr. Fossel.*] Now tell me who's coming.

MR. FOSSEL. I will, dear. Just sit down, and try not to get excited.

MRS. FOSSEL. All right, now I'm seated.

MR. FOSSEL. Well, of course, dear, you know I told you that the man who stole my watch phoned me today.

MRS. FOSSEL. Yes, you told me that.

MR. FOSSEL. Well, dear, there wasn't anything I could do but tell him to bring the watch here tonight and get the reward.

MRS. FOSSEL. You told him to come here?

MR. FOSSEL. Yes, dear, I had to.

MRS. FOSSEL. Good heavens, do you realize we may all be murdered?

MR. FOSSEL. Oh, nonsense, Mary. I talked to him today, and he didn't sound vicious—just slick, that's all.

MRS. FOSSEL. How did he know your phone number?

MR. FOSSEL. I put it in the advertisement.

MRS. FOSSEL. That certainly is bright, James, I must say. Now he knows where you work, and where you live, and he can hold you up either place, or both.

MR. FOSSEL. Oh, no, he couldn't, dear. He runs the risk now. We'll both see what he looks like, and we could have him arrested, if we wanted to.

MRS. FOSSEL. Then why don't you?

MR. FOSSEL. For the simple reason, dear, that my pride is hurt. Never in my life before has anyone been slick enough to pick my pocket. I have always been very sensitive to touch, and I can't understand how anyone could reach in my tight vest pocket and pull out that watch without my knowing it.

MRS. FOSSEL. Well, they did.

MR. FOSSEL. Yes, I know they did, and I'm so anxious to find out how that I'm going to give this crook ten dollars reward, instead of having him arrested.

MRS. FOSSEL. Didn't you tell him there would be no questions asked?

MR. FOSSEL. Yes, I did say that, but I'm hoping I can persuade him to show his cleverness.

MRS. FOSSEL. Cleverness! James, that's ridiculous. How could a creature low enough to pick pockets be clever?

MR. FOSSEL. Well, let's say slick then. It would take a pretty slick crook to pick my pocket.

MRS. FOSSEL. Oh, nonsense, I could pick it myself, if I wanted to do such a thing.

MR. FOSSEL. You just think you could. I'm sensitive to touch, I tell you. I always have been. When I was a youngster, the kids used to try to pull my handkerchief out of my pocket, without my knowing it, and they never could do it—and I still don't see how this fellow could.

MRS. FOSSEL. Maybe it's different with watches.

MR. FOSSEL. I don't see why it would be.

MRS. FOSSEL. So you're giving away ten dollars, just to find out how a crook works.

MR. FOSSEL. No, I'm giving five dollars to find how he works. The other five gets my watch back.

MRS. FOSSEL. Well, both fives will encourage this slick crook to be slicker. When he sees how gullible *you* are, he very likely will hold us all up, and take everything but Tillie.

MR. FOSSEL. Now, Mary, please. You know nothing's going to happen. If we can just be businesslike about it, everything will go very smoothly. Just keep Tillie outside, will you, and don't tell her anything. If you don't, she'll be sure to say some silly thing, or start yelling, and that might start trouble.

MRS. FOSSEL. Don't worry. I don't

MR. FOSSEL. Well, it won't be necessary. If we just keep calm, I can learn something, and get my watch back too. [*Mrs. Fossel looks at him with calm disgust. The doorbell rings at right.*] There he is now, I guess.

[*They both rise.*]

MRS. FOSSEL. Do you want Tillie to answer it?

MR. FOSSEL. No, please. You go, will you? She might spoil everything.

[*Mrs. Fossel hurries to door right and exits. Mr. Fossel takes a white envelope from his inside coat pocket, and inserts two five dollar bills. He then lays the envelope on the center table, and walks to a position facing the door right and waits. Mrs. Fossel ushers in Joe Kinney.*]

MRS. FOSSEL. This is Mr. Fossel.

MR. FOSSEL. Good evening, sir.

JOE. Evening.

MR. FOSSEL. You have the watch?

JOE. Yes.

[*He holds it out in his hand.*]

MR. FOSSEL. Well, I have the five dollars here too.

[*He walks toward table, and picks up the envelope, holding it in his hand.*]

JOE. Well, that's all there is to it, Mister. Here's your watch.

[*He hands it to Fossel.*]

MR. FOSSEL. [*lays the envelope back on the table. Mrs. Fossel crosses to a position in back of her husband, at stage left. Joe stands at right.*] Before we close this transaction, I wonder if I might ask a question.

JOE. [*takes a quick look around the room.*] You promised not to ask questions, Mister.

MR. FOSSEL. I know I did, but this isn't anything you wouldn't want to answer. I simply want to know how you got my watch.

MRS. FOSSEL. Don't be silly, James. You know how he got it; he stole it.

JOE. Listen, Lady, you stay out of this, if you know what's good for you. Nobody's going to say I stole your watch.

MR. FOSSEL. Mary, please keep quiet.

MRS. FOSSEL. Sorry.

MR. FOSSEL. [*to Joe.*] Just forget this interruption, will you, please? [*Joe nods sourly.*] It may sound silly to you, but I have always prided myself on the belief that I was too sensitive for anyone to pick my pocket. [*Joe smiles faintly.*] Now of course it's more than likely that you didn't get my watch that way, at all, but I just thought that—[*He hesitates.*] if you did, by any chance, you might be willing to tell me how you did it. [*He picks up the envelope from the table.*] I have an extra five dollars here—for that information.

JOE. Well, Mister, seein' as you're nice about it, I don't mind answering your question, especially as you're willing to pay five dollars for the answer. I'll start by saying that you ain't sensitive at all. It was very easy to take *your* watch from you.

MR. FOSSEL. Now would you mind showing me just how you did it?

JOE. Sure. I'll show you. [*He steps to stage center, downstage.*] Step right up here.

MR. FOSSEL. Certainly.

[*He takes a position to stage left of Joe, facing him.*]

JOE. Now put this in your vest pocket. [*He passes him the watch, which Mr. Fossel puts in his pocket.*] That's it. Now last Tuesday you was coming down town, on the elevated train, and it was very crowded. Remember?

MR. FOSSEL. Yes, I remember it being very crowded.

JOE. Well, you stood near the front of the train, see, like this—[*He lifts Mr. Fossel's arm into the air.*] and you was hanging on to a strap. Go on, hang on to it.

[*Mr. Fossel obeys, and grasps an imaginary strap.*]

MR. FOSSEL. [*sways.*] Oh, yes, I remember now.

[*Laughs.*]

JOE. In your other hand, see, you was holding a newspaper, and you kept your eyes right on it, like this— [*He bends Mr. Fossel's other arm, and puts it into a position as if holding a paper.*] Go on, look at it.

MR. FOSSEL. [*hastens to obey.*] Oh, yes, of course.

[*Mr. Fossel keeps swaying and looking at the supposed newspaper.*]

JOE. Now the train stops at the station, and I sees my chance. I brushes by you, like this— [*He presses the front of his body against Mr. Fossel's front and turns him around, laying his hand on his shoulder. Mr. Fossel faces upstage, as they pass, and Joe faces the audience.*] "Excuse me," I says, and you look at me. [*Mr. Fossel looks up at Joe, and their faces are close together.*] Remember that?

MR. FOSSEL. I think I do.

[*Joe now steps away to stage left.*]

JOE. Well, that's all there is to it, Mister. Here's your watch.

[*He holds it out to him. Mr. Fossel takes it.*]

MR. FOSSEL. [*with a dazed expression.*] Thank you. I can't understand it. I didn't feel you that time, either.

JOE. Of course you didn't. I didn't want you to.

MR. FOSSEL. Then I suppose I'm not sensitive at all.

JOE. No more'n an elephant, Mister.

MR. FOSSEL. [*dazed.*] I see.

JOE. Now I'll take that ten dollars, if you don't mind.

MR. FOSSEL. Oh, yes, certainly. Pass it to him, will you, Mary, please?

[*Mrs. Fossel takes the envelope from behind her.*]

MRS. FOSSEL. I have it right here. [*She opens the envelope and shows the bills.*] I'll seal them up if you don't mind. It'll prove we delivered them.

JOE. You needn't bother.

MRS. FOSSEL. It's no bother at all.

[*She turns her back to the audience, and seals the envelope from the front of the table.*]

MR. FOSSEL. [*to Joe.*] Well, sir, I guess that completes everything.

JOE. Yes, I guess it does. Good-bye.

[*He holds out his hand to Mr. Fossel.*]

MR. FOSSEL. Good-bye.

[*He walks up to the table.*]

MRS. FOSSEL. [*gives him the envelope.*] Here!

[*He takes it, and puts it in his inside pocket.*]

JOE. [*turns quickly to Mr. Fossel, as if trying to hold his attention.*] Listen, Mister—[*Mr. Fossel looks at him.*] Don't you worry about not being sensitive, as you call it. Your watch was lifted by an expert, Mister, and to an expert all suckers are easy, even the sensitive ones.

MR. FOSSEL. Yes, I guess they are.

[*Joe walks quickly to the door right and exits.*]

MRS. FOSSEL. You'd better look at your watch. The insides may be missing.

MR. FOSSEL. [*laughs.*] Oh, Mary, [*He puts his hand into*

his vest pocket, and his countenance changes. He cries out.]
Mary—he's taken it again! [*He runs to door right, calling.*]
Stop, thief!—Stop, thief!

MRS. FOSSEL. [*runs after him and grabs his arm.*] It's no
use, James. He's gone.

TILLIE. [*enters door right.*] Did you call, ma'am?

MRS. FOSSEL. Is that man still outside?

TILLIE. No, ma'am. He jumped in the car as if the old boy
was after him, and his friend in the car drove off. Is there
anything wrong?

MRS. FOSSEL. No Tillie, it's all right. [*Mr. Fossel stands
dazed and says nothing.*] Just leave us alone, please. I'll call
you when we're ready.

TILLIE. Yes, ma'am.

[*She exits right.*]

MRS. FOSSEL. [*to Mr. Fossel.*] Now come over here and sit
down. [*She leads the way to the couch stage left.*] That's all
you can do.

[*They sit down, Mr. Fossel at left, Mrs. Fossel at his
right.*]

MR. FOSSEL. [*bitterly.*] The dirty crook! He took my
watch and my ten dollars too.

MRS. FOSSEL. Oh, no, he didn't. I have the ten dollars
right here.

[*She takes them from her dress front and holds them up
to him.*]

MR. FOSSEL. [*in great delight.*] Oh, Mary, you angel. How
did you do it?

MRS. FOSSEL. [*in a harsh voice.*] You promised not to ask
questions, mister.

MR. FOSSEL. Go on. Tell me.—Please.

MRS. FOSSEL. Well, while you talked, I sealed the letter. Before I did it, however, I took out the two fives and sealed up a laundry bill that I found on the table.

MR. FOSSEL. Mary! How clever!

MRS. FOSSEL. Well, I had to do something. No miserable pickpocket is going to cheat me, if I can help it.

MR. FOSSEL. You're a wonder, Mary. Now let me have the ten, will you?

MR. FOSSEL. [*smiles.*] Say, wait a moment. Shouldn't I get some reward too?

MR. FOSSEL. Why, Mary, do you want to be paid for your good deed?

MRS. FOSSEL. No, I don't expect to be paid, exactly, but you might encourage me a little by giving me the ten for a new hat.

MR. FOSSEL. You deserve to win it, I suppose, and I deserve to lose it.

[*The door opens and Tillie enters, door right.*]

TILLIE. Dinner's ready, ma'am.

MRS. FOSSEL. [*turns her head and looks over back of couch.*] Go on out, Tillie, will you? We're not ready yet.

TILLIE. All right, ma'am, but I'm afraid it'll be spoilt.

[*She exits right.*]

MRS. FOSSEL. [*Mr. Fossel looks up at her and she smiles down at him.*] Let it spoil. It isn't important right now. [*She pulls his head over on her shoulder and lays her head against his.*] Now close your eyes, dear, and relax. We're not going to eat for five minutes yet.

MR. FOSSEL. [*he does as she requests.*] Thanks, Mary.

MRS. FOSSEL. Sh.—Don't think about a thing. [*She takes the ten dollars which she has in her hand and very deftly pushes it into his vest pocket, watching him closely to see if he notices. He still keeps his eyes closed.*] That's it, just relax. Everything's going to be all right.

[*She gives a big sigh, and lays her head against his again.*]

CURTAIN

THE FINGER OF GOD

(Revised)

by PERCIVAL WILDE

Taken from *Dawn and Other One-Act Plays,* this revised short study deals dramatically with a speculator who reverses his evil designs under the influence of a girl.

Percival Wilde has had varied experiences as bank-clerk, book-reviewer, and writer-director of one-act plays. Because his technique is masterly and his characters human, his plays have enjoyed great popularity both here and abroad, especially in England. His *Craftsmanship of the One-Act Play* is a guide to aspiring playwrights.

PERCIVAL WILDE

THE FINGER OF GOD

CHARACTERS

STRICKLAND

BENSON

A GIRL

SCENE: Living-room of Strickland's apartment.

TIME: A cold night in winter, about 10:30

The living room of Strickland's apartment. At the right a door leads to the exterior, and a second door, leading to another room, may, if desired, be placed in the rear wall, to the right. A mantel, under which is a fireplace, is at the rear, c. In the L. wall is a large recessed window, heavily curtained.

The furnishings, in general, are luxurious and costly. Central among them is an ornate writing desk, upon which is a telephone.

[As the curtain rises, STRICKLAND, *seated at the desk, is glancing through papers, which he destroys and consigns to a wastebasket at his elbow. It is night: ten-thirty by the clock on the mantel; a cold night in winter.* BENSON *enters, carrying a large suitcase, which he puts down at once.]*

STRICKLAND. Benson!

BENSON. Yes, sir.

STRICKLAND. Close the window: it's cold.

BENSON. [*goes to the window.*] The window *is* closed, sir. It's been closed all evening.

STRICKLAND. [*after a pause.*] Benson.

BENSON. Yes, sir?

STRICKLAND. Don't forget a heavy overcoat.

BENSON. I've put it in already, sir.

STRICKLAND. Plenty of fresh linen?

BENSON. Yes, sir.

STRICKLAND. Collars and ties?

BENSON. I've looked out for everything, sir.

STRICKLAND. [*after a pause.*] You sent off the trunks this afternoon?

BENSON. Yes, sir.

STRICKLAND. You're sure they can't be traced?

BENSON. I had one truck take them to a vacant lot, and another take them to the station.

STRICKLAND. Good!

BENSON. [*at the left of the desk.*] I checked them through to Chicago. Here are the checks. [*He hands them over.*] What train do we take, sir?

STRICKLAND. *I* take the midnight. You follow me some time next week. We mustn't be seen leaving town together.

BENSON. How will I find you in Chicago?

STRICKLAND. You won't. You'll take a room somewhere, and I'll take rooms somewhere else till it's all blown over. When I want you I'll put an ad in the *Tribune*.

BENSON. You don't know when that will be, sir?

STRICKLAND. As soon as I think it is safe. It may be two weeks. It may be a couple of months. But you will stay in Chicago till you read the ad. You understand?

BENSON. Yes, sir.

STRICKLAND. Have you plenty of money?

BENSON. Not enough to last a couple of months.

STRICKLAND. [*producing a large pocketbook.*] How much do you want?

BENSON. Five or six hundred.

STRICKLAND. [*takes out a few bills. Stops.*] Wait a minute! I left that much in my bureau drawer.

[*He goes toward the door.*]

BENSON. Mr. Strickland?

STRICKLAND. Yes?

BENSON. It's the midnight train for Chicago, isn't it?

STRICKLAND. Yes.

[*He goes into the next room.*]

BENSON. [*waits an instant. Then he seats himself at the desk, lifts the telephone receiver, and dials.*] Hello . . . Hello. This Finley? This is Benson. . . . He's going to take the midnight train for Chicago. Pennsylvania Railroad. You had better arrest him at the station. If he once gets to Chicago you'll never find him. And, Finley, you won't forget *me*, will you? . . . I want five thousand dollars for it. Yes, five thousand. That's little enough. He's got almost three hundred thousand on him, and you won't turn in *all* of that to Headquarters. Yes, it's cash. Large bills. [STRICKLAND's *step is heard.*] Midnight for Chicago.

[BENSON *hangs up the receiver and rises in leisurely fashion as* STRICKLAND *re-enters.*]

STRICKLAND. Here's your money, Benson. Count it.

BENSON. [*after counting.*] Six hundred dollars, thank you, sir. [*He crosses to the* R.] Shall I go now?

STRICKLAND. No. Wait a minute. [*He goes to the telephone and dials.*] Hello . . . Pennsylvania? I want a stateroom for Chicago, midnight train. Yes, tonight.

BENSON. [*moving toward him.*] Don't give your own name, sir.

STRICKLAND. No. The name is Stevens. . . . Oh, you have one reserved in that name already? Well, this is *Alfred* Stevens. . . . You have it reserved in that name? Then give me another stateroom. . . . What? You haven't any other? [*He pauses in an instant's thought. Then decisively.*] Never mind, then. Good-by. [*He turns to* BENSON.] Benson, go right down to the Pennsylvania, and get the stateroom that is reserved for Alfred Stevens. You've got to get there before he does. Wait for me at the train gate.

BENSON. Yes, sir.

STRICKLAND. Don't waste any time. I'll see you later.

BENSON. Very well, sir.

[*He takes up the suitcase, and goes.*]

STRICKLAND. [*left alone, opens drawer after drawer of the desk systematically, destroying what few papers are still left. He stops suddenly, as if hearing something; stops again as there is a knock at the door. He pauses, very much startled. A little wait, and then the knock, a single knock, is repeated. He rises, goes to the door, opens it.*] Who's there?

A GIRL. I, sir. [*She enters. She is young: certainly under thirty: perhaps under twenty-five: possibly still younger. A somewhat shabby boa of some dark fur encircles her neck, and makes her pallid face stand out with startling distinctness from beneath a mass of lustrous hair. She is ethereal; frail; not too well dressed; but* STRICKLAND *has no time to observe her appearance. He greets her with a volley of questions.*]

STRICKLAND. Who are you?

THE GIRL. Why, don't you remember me, sir?

STRICKLAND. No.

THE GIRL. I'm from the office, sir.

STRICKLAND. The office?

THE GIRL. *Your* office. I'm one of your personal stenographers, sir.

STRICKLAND. Oh. I suppose I didn't recognize you on account of the hat. What do you want?

THE GIRL. There were some letters which came late this afternoon——

STRICKLAND. [*interrupting harshly.*] And you're bothering me with them now? [*He crosses to the door, and holds it open.*] I've got no time. Good night.

THE GIRL. [*timidly.*] I thought you'd want to see these letters.

STRICKLAND. Plenty of time tomorrow.

THE GIRL. But you won't be here tomorrow, will you?

STRICKLAND. [*starting violently.*] Won't be here? What do you mean?

THE GIRL. You're taking the train to Chicago tonight.

STRICKLAND. How did you know—— [*He stops himself. Then, with forced ease.*] Taking a train to Chicago? Of course not! What put that idea in your head?

THE GIRL. Why, you told me, sir.

STRICKLAND. *I* told you?

THE GIRL. You said so this afternoon.

STRICKLAND. [*harshly.*] I didn't see you this afternoon!

THE GIRL. [*without contradicting him.*] No sir? [*She produces a timetable.*] Then I found this timetable. [*She holds it out. He snatches it.*]

STRICKLAND. Where did you find it?

THE GIRL. On your desk, sir.

STRICKLAND. On my desk?

THE GIRL. Yes, sir.

STRICKLAND. [*suddenly and directly.*] You're lying!

THE GIRL. Why, Mr. Strickland!

STRICKLAND. This timetable never reached my desk! I lost

it between the railroad station and my office.

THE GIRL. Did you, sir? But it's the same timetable: you see, you checked the midnight train. [*He looks at her suspiciously.*] I reserved a stateroom for you.

STRICKLAND. [*astonished.*] You reserved a stateroom?

THE GIRL. [*smiling.*] I knew you'd forget it. You have your head so full of other things. So I telephoned as soon as you left the office.

STRICKLAND. [*biting his lip angrily.*] I suppose you made the reservation in my own name?

THE GIRL. No, sir.

STRICKLAND. [*immensely surprised.*] What?

THE GIRL. I thought you'd prefer some other name: you didn't want your trip to be known.

STRICKLAND. No, I didn't. [*A good deal startled, he looks at her as if he were about to ask, "How did you know that?" She returns his gaze unflinchingly. The question remains unasked. But a sudden thought strikes him.*] What name did you give?

THE GIRL. Stevens, sir.

STRICKLAND. [*thunderstruck.*] Stevens?

THE GIRL. Alfred Stevens.

STRICKLAND. [*gasping.*] What made you choose that name?

THE GIRL. I don't know, sir.

STRICKLAND. You don't *know?*

THE GIRL. No, sir. It was just the first name that popped into my head. I said "Stevens," and when the clerk asked for the first name, I said "Alfred."

STRICKLAND. [*after a pause.*] Have you ever *known* anybody of that name?

THE GIRL. No, sir.

STRICKLAND. [*with curious insistence.*] You are *sure* you never knew anybody of that name?

THE GIRL. How can I be sure? I may have; I don't remember.

STRICKLAND. [*abruptly.*] How old are you? [*He gives her no time to answer.*] You're not twenty, are you?

THE GIRL. [*smiling.*] Do you think so?

STRICKLAND. [*continuing the current of his thoughts.*] And I'm forty-seven. It was more than twenty-five years ago . . . You couldn't have known.

THE GIRL. [*after a pause.*] No, sir.

STRICKLAND. [*looking at her with something of fear in his eye.*] What is your name?

THE GIRL. Does it matter? You didn't recognize my *face* a few minutes ago; my *name* can't mean much to you. I'm just one of the office force: I'm the girl who answers when you push the button three times. [*She opens a handbag.*] These are the letters I brought with me.

STRICKLAND. [*crossing to the L., not offering to take them.*] What are they about?

THE GIRL. [*opening the first and following him.*] This is from a woman who wants to invest some money.

STRICKLAND. How much?

THE GIRL. Only a thousand dollars.

STRICKLAND. Why didn't you turn it over to the clerks?

THE GIRL. "The savings of a lifetime," she writes.

STRICKLAND. [*at the window.*] What of it?

THE GIRL. She wrote that she had confidence in you. She says that she wants you to invest it for her yourself.

STRICKLAND. You shouldn't have bothered me with that.

[*He pauses.*] Did she enclose the money?

THE GIRL. Yes. A certified check.

[*She hands it over to him.*]

STRICKLAND. [*taking the check, and putting it in his pocketbook.*] Write her—oh, you know what to write, that I will give the matter my personal attention.

THE GIRL. Yes, sir. She says she doesn't want a big return on her investment. She wants something that will be perfectly safe, and she knows you will take care of her.

STRICKLAND. Yes. Of course. What else have you?

THE GIRL. A dozen other letters like it.

STRICKLAND. All from old women?

THE GIRL. [*seriously.*] Some of them. Here is one from a young man who has saved a little money. He says that when he gets a little more he's going to open a store, and go into business for himself. Here is another from a girl whose husband was killed at Korea. She wants you to invest the insurance. Here is another from—but they're all pretty much alike.

STRICKLAND. Why did you bring them here?

THE GIRL. Every one of these letters asks you to do the investing yourself.

STRICKLAND. Oh!

THE GIRL. And you're leaving town tonight. Here are the checks. [*She passes them over.*] Every one of them is made out to you personally; not to the firm.

STRICKLAND. [*after a pause.*] You shouldn't have come here. . . . [*He crosses to the right of* C.] I haven't time to bother with that sort of thing. Every man who has five dollars to invest asks the head of the firm to attend to it himself. It means nothing. I get hundreds of letters like those.

THE GIRL. Still——

STRICKLAND. What?

THE GIRL. You must do something to deserve such letters or they wouldn't keep on coming in. [*She smiles.*] It's a wonderful thing to inspire such confidence in people!

STRICKLAND. Do you think so?

THE GIRL. It is more than wonderful! It is magnificent! These people don't know you from Adam. Not one in a hundred has seen you: not one in a thousand calls you by your first name. But they've all heard of you: you're as real to them as if you were a member of their family. And what is even more real than you is your reputation, something in which they rest their absolute confidence, something in which they place their implicit trust!

STRICKLAND. [*turning slowly to the girl.*] So you think there are few honest men?

THE GIRL. No; there are many of them. But there is something about you that is different: something in the tone of your voice: something in the way you shake hands: something in the look of your eye, that is reassuring. There is never a doubt—never a question about you. Oh, it's splendid! Simply splendid! [*She pauses.*] What a satisfaction it must be to you to walk along the street and know that everyone you meet must say to himself, "There goes an honest man!" It's been such an inspiration to me!

STRICKLAND. To *you?*

THE GIRL. Oh, I know that I'm just one of the office force to you. You don't even know my name. But you don't imagine that anyone can see you as I have seen you, can work with you as I have worked with you, without there being *some* kind of an effect? You know, in my own troubles——

STRICKLAND. [*interrupting.*] So you have troubles?

THE GIRL. You don't pay me a very big salary, and there are others whom I must help. But I'm not complaining. [*She smiles.*] I—I used to be like the other girls. I used to watch the clock. I used to count the hours and the minutes till the day's work was over. But it's different now.

STRICKLAND. [*slowly.*] How—different?

THE GIRL. I thought it over, and I made up my mind that it wasn't right to count the minutes you worked for an honest man. [STRICKLAND *turns away.*] And there is a new pleasure in my work: I do my best—that's all I can do, but *you* do your best, and it's the *least* I can do.

STRICKLAND. [*after a pause, moving back of the desk, and sitting.*] Are you sure—I do my best? Are you sure I am an honest man?

THE GIRL. Don't you know it yourself, Mr. Strickland?

STRICKLAND. [*after another pause.*] You remember—a few minutes ago, you spoke the name of Alfred Stevens?

THE GIRL. Yes.

STRICKLAND. Suppose I told you that there once *was* an Alfred Stevens? [THE GIRL *does not answer.*] Suppose I told you that Stevens stole money—stole it when there was no excuse for it—when he didn't need it. But the chance came, and he couldn't resist the temptation. . . . He was eighteen years old then.

THE GIRL. [*gently.*] Only a boy.

STRICKLAND. Only a boy, yes, but he had the dishonest streak in him! Other boys passed by the same opportunity. Stevens didn't even know what to do with the money when he had stolen it. They caught him in less than twenty-four hours. It was almost funny.

THE GIRL. He was punished?

STRICKLAND. [*nodding.*] He served a year in jail. God!

What a year! His folks wouldn't do a thing for him: they said such a thing had never happened in the family. And they let him take the consequences. [*He pauses.*} When he got out— [*stopping to correct himself*] —when he was *let* out, his people offered him help. But he was too proud to accept: help hadn't been offered when he needed it most. He told his family that he never wanted to see them again. He changed his name so they couldn't find him. He left his home town. He came here.

THE GIRL. And he has been honest ever since!

STRICKLAND. Ever since: for twenty-eight years! It was hard at times, terribly hard! In the beginning, when he had to go hungry and cold, when he saw other men riding around in automobiles, he wondered if he hadn't made a mistake. He had knocked about a good deal; he had learned a lot, and he wouldn't have been caught so easily the second time. It was *almost* worth taking the chance! It was *almost* worth getting a foot of lead pipe, and waiting in some dark street, waiting, waiting for some sleek *honest* man with his pockets full of money! It would have been so simple! And he knew *how!* I don't know why he didn't do it.

THE GIRL. Tell me more.

STRICKLAND. He managed to live. It wasn't pleasant living: it wasn't even decent living, but he stayed alive! He had thought the year in jail was terrible. The first year he was free was worse. He had never been hungry in jail.

THE GIRL. Then his chance came.

STRICKLAND. Yes, it *was* a chance. He found a purse in the gutter, and he returned it to the owner before he had made up his mind whether to keep it or not. So they said he was honest! He knew he wasn't! And when the expected reward turned out to be a job, he worked—worked because he was afraid not to work—worked so that he wouldn't have any time to think, because he knew that if he began to think, he would begin to steal! Then they said he was a hard worker, and they promoted him: they made him manager. That gave him more chances to steal, but there were so many men watching him, so many men anxious for him to make a slip so that they might climb over him, that he didn't dare.

[*He pauses.*]

THE GIRL. And then?

STRICKLAND. The rest was easy. He didn't steal because he knew they'd catch him. [*He pauses again.*] But he wasn't honest at bottom! The rotten streak was still there! After twenty-eight years things began to be bad. He speculated: lost all the money he could call his own, and made up his mind to take other money that *wasn't* his own, all he could lay his hands on, and run off with it! It was wrong! It was the work of a lifetime gone to pieces! But it was the rottenness in him coming to the surface! It was the thief he thought dead coming to life again!

THE GIRL. [*after a pause.*] What a pity!

STRICKLAND. He had been honest so long—he had made other people think that he was honest so long, that he had made *himself* think that he was honest!

THE GIRL. Was he wrong, Mr. Strickland?

STRICKLAND. [*looking into her eyes; very quietly.*] Stevens, please. [*There is a long pause. He rises.*] I don't know what sent you: who sent you: but you've come here tonight as I am running away. You're too late. You can't stop me. Not even the finger of God himself could stop me! I've gone too far. [*He goes on in a voice which is low, but terrible in its earnestness.*] Here is money! [*He pulls out his pocketbook and empties it on the desk.*] Hundreds of thousands of it, not a cent of it mine! And I'm stealing it, do you understand me? *Stealing* it! Tomorrow the firm will be bankrupt, and there'll be a reward out for me. [*He smiles grimly and bows.*] Here, if you please, is your honest man! What have you to say to him?

THE GIRL. [*very quietly.*] The man who has been honest so long that he has made *himself* think that he is honest *can't* steal!

STRICKLAND. [*hoarsely.*] You believe *that?*

THE GIRL. [*opening her bag again.*] I was left a little money this week: only a few hundred dollars, hardly enough to bother you with. Will you take care of it for me—Alfred Stevens?

STRICKLAND. Good God!

[*And utterly unnerved he collapses to a chair. There is a long pause.*]

THE GIRL. [*crossing slowly to the window, and drawing aside the curtain.*] Look! What a beautiful night! The thousands of sleeping houses! The millions of shining stars! And the lights beneath! And in the distance, how the stars and the lights meet! So that one cannot say here God ends; here Man begins.

[*The telephone rings harshly, and shrilly.* STRICKLAND *goes to the receiver.*]

STRICKLAND. [*quietly.*] Yes, Benson? . . . You're afraid I'm going to miss the train? . . . Yes? Well, I'm *going* to miss the train! . . . I'm going to stay and face the music! [*Hysterically.*] I'm an honest man, d'ye hear me? I'm an honest man! [*And furiously, he pitches the telephone to the door, and stands panting, shivering, on the spot. From the window a soft radiance beckons, and trembling in every limb, putting out his hands as if to ward off some unseen obstacle, he moves there slowly.*] Did you hear what I told him? I'm going to make good. I'm going to face the music! Because I'm an honest man! An honest man!

[*He gasps, stops abruptly, and in a sudden panic-stricken movement, tears the curtains down. The window is closed—has never been opened—but the girl has vanished. And as* STRICKLAND, *burying his face in his hands, drops to his knees in awe, the curtain falls.*]

CURTAIN

THE OWL AND TWO YOUNG MEN

by

E. P. CONKLE

From *Loolie and Other Short Plays* comes this miniature sketch of youngsters from the hills of Peru, Nebraska. Conkle's folks show quizzical traits or heroic virtues.

The author made his reputation with his first collection of Western sketches, *Crick Bottom Plays,* shot through with colloquial vigor and poetry. Many of his plays have been shown in community and college theatres across the country.

THE OWL AND TWO YOUNG MEN

CHARACTERS

JIM PURDUE

JERRY PROCTER

A moon. A log. A well-curb with an owl on top. Low shrubs and brush. The silence of the night.

[JIM PURDUE, *thirteen, pushes his way in Right. He wears overalls and a torn hat. He is barefoot. He lags over to the log. He sits on it, chin in hand.* JERRY PROCTER *enters up Left. He is, also, thirteen and in overalls. A cap hangs to the back of his head. He is barefoot. Without much noticing* JIM, *he, too, drops onto the log, head in hand.*]

JIM. Howdy.

JERRY. Howdy.

[*Both* BOYS *fumble in their pockets. Each takes out a small, dainty handkerchief. Each looks at the white bit of cloth, and sighs. The owl hoots. Both* BOYS *look hastily toward it, stuffing their handkerchiefs back into their pockets.*]

JIM. Perty good weather.

JERRY. If it keeps up.

JIM. Goin' to rain?

JERRY. Might. Could git fishworms if it should.

JIM. Me and Tom got a couple-a croppies.[1]

JERRY. Over behind the hog-waller?[2]

JIM. They was scrumptious.

[*Silence.*]

JERRY. You got your 'rithmetic for tomorrow?

JIM. The third one's got fractions.

[1] Fresh-water fish.
[2] A place where hogs huddle.

JERRY. Fractions is easy. All you got to do is to—divide. Or something.

JIM. Sometimes you got to minus. If you're a mind to. Like when you take two from something you don't git nothin'.

JERRY. You git a—ought.

JIM. No, you don't. You don't git nothin'.

JERRY. Nothin's—ought.

JIM. Ought's—zero.

JERRY. Then ain't nothin' ought?

JIM. Mebby so. It's a goose-egg any way you lay it. It don't mean a derned thing to me, no-ways. Fractions is bug-bears.

JERRY. They are grizzly-bears. [*The* BOYS *turn to the moon at Right, sigh, and drop their heads.*] Is—Tom goin' with Rosy Gay?

JIM. Stronger than horsereddish.

JERRY. I don't see how a feller can git stuck on no woman.

JIM. Women is regular cyclones.

JERRY. Best thing is not to have nothin' to do with them.

JIM. I never tech one—lessn I'm shoved beside her.

JERRY. A feller ort to be powerful and resist 'em, I s'pose.

JIM. I s'pose *so*. [*Both* BOYS *straighten up.*] When he can.

JERRY. If he can. [*Silence. The* BOYS· *drop into deeper thoughts.*] What you s'pose love is?

JIM. It's a—hankerin'?

JERRY. A—hankerin'?

JIM. Like when you got your eye on a pair-a skates and you can't git your hands onto 'em.

JERRY. It sure nicks a feller.

JIM. Made a plumb fool out-a Tom.

JERRY. Hain't made no fool out-a me. So far.

JIM. Me, neither.

JERRY. When it gits a feller, it gits him down.

JIM. Feels plumb tuckered out[1] all the blessed time.

JERRY. Ain't no good for to wipe your feet on, even.

JIM. All the time imaginin' things.

JERRY. Sometimes the derndest things.

JIM. Usually are.

JERRY. It's—awful!

JIM. I never seen the likes-a it! [BOTH *sigh.*] You—ever been in love?

JERRY. Have—you?

JIM. Kind-a.

JERRY. Me—too.

JIM. But not more'n knee-deep.

JERRY. I was up to my waist, onct. I never lost my head yet, though.

JIM. I almost lost my watch, onct.

JERRY. The one your Pa give you?

JIM. Yeh.

JERRY. Where—is it at?

JIM. It's—over home. [*Pause.*] Where's your frog-stabber at?

JERRY. Over in my bedroom. I don't carry it no more—either.

JIM. Me—neither.

JERRY. Girl might git it away from a feller—[BOTH *fumble with their handkerchiefs*]—if he wasn't careful.

JIM. She'd sure try to—even if she couldn't cut the mustard.

---

[1] tired out

JERRY. Prob'ly do it, if she took a feller unawares.

JIM. Us men can sure be derned fools, can't we?

JERRY. Who—you a derned fool for now, Jim?

JIM. Oh—I got a peach in mind right now.

JERRY. Me—too. I ain't sayin' who.

JIM. I ain't either. But mine's about all a feller could expect.

JERRY. Mine's sure all there! She's got eyes, and teeth, and hands——

JIM. So's—mine! Her eyes is blue—— [*They* BOTH *dream.*] Her hands is little——

JERRY. So's her heart——

JIM. You can hear it beatin' somewheres.

JERRY. Ain't it sure tough?

[*Silence.*]

JIM. We was standing over there by the well-curb.

JERRY. Us—too.

[JIM *gets up and goes to the well.* JERRY *follows and stands opposite.*]

JIM. —standin'——

JERRY. —leanin'——

[*They* BOTH *lean on the curb.* BOTH *look down at a red heart drawn on the boards with crayon. They sigh.*]

JIM. That's—her heart.

JERRY. It's—hern.

[*They look at one another.*]

JIM. That's my girl's heart! She put it there special for me!

JERRY. It's my girl's heart! She drawed it fer only me!

JIM. She told me three nights ago she didn't hanker after nobody but me!

JERRY. She told me I was her moon and stars!

JIM. She told me I was her little X. Y. Z.

JERRY. Who is your girl, anyways?

JIM. Who's yourn?

JERRY. Vivie's—mine.

JIM. She's—mine.

[*Both* BOYS *stop for breath, dumbfounded and glowering.*]

JERRY. How do you git that-a-way?

JIM. How do you, yourse'f?

JERRY. She ain't yourn!

JIM. She is so!

JERRY. You're a fibber!

JIM. You're a tattle-taler!

JERRY. Our youngens is to be called Mary, and Dill, and Orthy, and 'Phelia.

JIM. Them is my names!

JERRY. Yourn? How come?

JIM. I'm—their Pa, ain't I?

JERRY. In a pig's eye!

JIM. Yeh. And in a calf's-knuckle!

JERRY. We planned out a house for us.

JIM. So did we! Down in Cherry Medders.

JERRY. That's—ourn!

JIM. It's—ourn!

JERRY. What you got to buy a house with anywheres at? Exceptin' a hog-house.

JIM. What you got? You couldn't even buy a hog-house!

JERRY. I got two nickels and a horseshoe tag.

JIM. Pooh! I got an old binder my Pa give me.

JERRY. Yeh—and looky what she let me have, too!

JIM. Yeh—and looky what she let me have to use, too!

[BOTH *pull out their handkerchiefs. They are identical.*]

JERRY. I lent her my watch to keep till we could git us a 'larum clock.

JIM. I donated her my frog-stabber[1] to cut up her vittels with after we're married.

JERRY. I—I—I'll fight—you! I'll fight you, I will! I got my honor to withhold!

JIM. I—I—I'll fight you! I reckon I can pertect my women-folks from men of your stripe!

JERRY. You are a—a—a back-biter!

JIM. You are a—a—a belly-buster!

JERRY. Don't you call me nothin' else, or I'll—I'll—*I'll!*

JIM. I'll shove you into the middle of next week if you say another word against me or mine!

JERRY. Yourn—pooh!

JIM. Yourn—pooh! [BOTH *walk around.*] If I was you I'd go and roll over and die!

JERRY. Looks to me like you already had! I—I—I can't tolerate you none!

JIM. I never could—you! You ain't warshed your feet for a coon's-age!

JERRY. You tryin' to insult me? I wash 'em every year! I'll —fight you a—duel!

JIM. You can't buffalo me! I'm hard-hearted!

. JERRY. I almost et a nail onct! I'll—fight you a duel!

JIM. I heard you the first time. I ain't sayin' I won't do it, am I?

JERRY. You're quiverin' inside your pants.

---

[1] probably a farm tool

JIM. That's the wind a-blowin' up 'em.

JERRY. I never fit[1] a duel before, but I'll fit one onct—for her!

JIM. I've fit lots of 'em. I almost killed a cow onct fittin' one.

JERRY. Well—if you say so.

JIM. The first thing a person does is to peel off their coats.

JERRY. I reckon a feller don't haf to peel off their pants, does he?

JIM. Well, he could. [JERRY *gets his coat off.* JIM *follows suit.* JERRY *rolls up his overalls.*] What you rollin' up your legs for?

JERRY. So's I can—run.

JIM. Run?

JERRY. After I knock the sap out-a you!

JIM. I'm goin' to knock the socks off-a you!

JERRY. I ain't got no socks on—so there! You—all set?

JIM. I'm waitin'. We got to pace off.

JERRY. Pace what off?

JIM. Ten paces—turn—and biff!

JERRY. Backs to backs. [*They stand back to back.*] You—all set to pace?

JIM. Yeh. And see you don't go to trottin'. When I take my tenth step, you better'd look to your pussonal self!

JERRY. You got a mess to worry about yourse'f!

JIM. It's the revival of the fittinest! I'm fittin' for my good name!

JERRY. So'm I! My Ma's name wasn't tarnished. My Pa's was a few times, but——

JIM. You—all set?

[1] fought

JERRY. Are——you?

JIM. Let's—go!

JERRY. Where to?

JERRY. Straight forward. I'll count the paces.

JERRY. I will myse'f.

JIM. Both of us will.

JERRY. If you can count that far.

JIM. I counted to a million onct. When I was countin' the number-a lies you told!

JERRY. Nobody could count the many you told!

[*The* BOYS *get set back to back. They begin to pace.*]

BOTH. One!

JERRY. You—started to agitate?

JIM. I ain't suckin' my thumb on a stump!

BOTH. Two! Three! Four! Five!

JIM. I ain't goin' to be responsible for your corpse!

JERRY. When I'm a corpse you'll be a carcass!

BOTH. Six! Seven! Eight! Nine! Ten! [BOTH *make simultaneous movements for guns, pistols, or swords. They have none. In desperation they turn upon each other open-mouthed.*]. I ain't—you ain't—we ain't got no—weapons!

[*The owl hoots.*]

JIM. Shut up, old owl!

JERRY. A owl ain't got good sense. He's always p'tendin'.

JIM. How—we goin' to duel this out?

JERRY. We got to settle it on the field-a battle.

JIM. We can't both marry her!

JERRY. It'd be—bigamy!

JIM. Ain't goin' to pile myse'f into no—bigamy!

JERRY. Wouldn't be satisfactory on neither side.

JIM. We could—throw rocks!

JERRY. Be mighty hard to kill ourse'fs with a—rock.

JIM. Was we to peck each other on the noodles, we'd go home bawlin' our eyes out.

JERRY. I'd just as soon throw a wagon-load of rocks at you!

JIM. Dare you to touch me so much as with a weeny pebble!

JERRY. Is it a—dare?

JIM. I ain't sayin' *is it* or *ain't it*. I'm just sayin' *shall it been!*

JERRY. I won't take that off-a nobody. Not even a duke!

JIM. You ain't real bright, are you?

JERRY. Dag-gone you! Come on!

JIM. Dag-gone you!

JERRY. You coudn't hit a barn-door!

JIM. You couldn't hit the derned barn itse'f!

JERRY. You—insultin' me?

JIM. I'm a-tryin' to!

JERRY. Dag-gone *you!*

JIM. Dag-gone *you!*

[*The* BOYS *begin to pile up their ammunition—rocks, stones, pebbles, and a few twigs and broken limbs of trees and leaves. As they do this, a* BOY *and* GIRL *appear on the hill in the rear silhouetted against the moon. They are lovers.*]

JERRY. I hate you like rotten tomaters! Just wait till I git all my ammunish!

JIM. You're blacker than a blasted stump! If you git her it'll be over my shirt-tail!

JERRY. I'll git her! And you won't have no shirt-tail left when I git over you! Grrrrrr!

JIM. Grrrrrr!

[*They start to throw. Then the owl hoots. The* BOYS *stop and look up. The* GIRL *laughs. The* BOYS *turn. They stare. The* GIRL *laughs again. They drop their stones and look at one another. They speak in hoarse whispers as they come together.*]

JERRY. It's—her!

JIM. It's—her!

JERRY. And—Tom!

JIM. And—Tom!

BOTH. We've been—treasoned!

JIM. She's sparkin' Tom tonight!

JERRY. What're us fellers goin' to do?

JIM. We got to hang together, now!

JERRY. Got to settle Tom's hash for him! Steppin' his ornery[1] foot into our fracas!

JERRY. They'll be Tom's little Marys, and Dills, and Orthys, and 'Phelias if we don't look out!

JIM. She's went and back-slid on us, Jerry!

JERRY. Let's throw clods at 'em, Jim!

JIM. Tom ain't nothin' but a derned wart!

JERRY. He's a blamed old bunion! You—got any clods?

JIM. Yeh. I'm gittin' my arms full. We'll put 'em in our handkerchiefses!

[BOTH *get on their knees and gather up their ammunition. They get out their handkerchiefs, with great misgivings, and fill them with pebbles. Then they get up.*]

JERRY. The one she give me wasn't clean. Let's count ten.

JIM. When we git to ten, then we'll——

[*Getting clods,* BOTH.]

[1] mean, vile

BOTH. Let 'er flicker!

[*They begin throwing. The* COUPLE *gets up and runs away. The* BOYS *follow, throwing and laughing at their fun. The owl hoots.*]

CURTAIN

LOVE IN THE APE HOUSE

by F. SLADEN-SMITH

Here is a laughable situation treated in fresh and youthful vein and streaked with wit and satire.

The author, F. Sladen-Smith, is a producer, playwright, and critic. Most of his plays have been written for the Unnamed Theatre of Manchester, England.

F. SLADEN-SMITH
BRITISH CRITIC AND PLAYWRIGHT.

LOVE IN THE APE HOUSE

By F. Sladen-Smith

CHARACTERS

FLORRIE

HERBERT

CLARENCE

AN APE

The scene is a secluded part of a Monkey House in which is kept a large Ape. The back of the stage is not unlike a small but perfectly plain proscenium, the large, square opening in the centre containing vertical bars through which the Ape is dimly seen. The wall on either side of the cage is pasted with notices concerning times of closing, feeding of the animals, etc., as well as various warnings, and in the centre of the short wall, which runs across on a level with the bottom of the cage, is an impressive inscription with the name of the animal and its characteristics. In front of the cage, and a little lower than the wall at the back, is a long seat such as is seen in parks, and on the right and left are walls containing large entrances without doors, obviously leading to other parts of the monkey house.

The light, which is supposed to come from windows opposite the seat, is that of a summer afternoon.

FLORRIE *and* HERBERT *enter left, both in their best clothes and evidently out for the day.*

FLORRIE. [*hanging on to* HERBERT'S *arm.*] My word, Herbert, I *am* enjoying myself! All them funny animals, birds and fishes. And don't it make you confused? I bet you I couldn't tell the difference now between a lion and an alba-

67

tross if you asked me. [*She sees the seat.*] No use making a
toil of a pleasure. Let's sit down. [*They sit together;* FLORRIE
L., HERBERT R. FLORRIE *looks behind her and sees the* APE.]
O—o! look at that!

HERBERT. [*with explanatory condescension.*] That's an ape,
that is. Supposed to be like us, an ape is.

FLORRIE. [*surveying the* APE.] Well, it has a look of Uncle
Joshua, I will say that. That's just the way he used to eat at
Chapel teas. [*Becoming more attracted.*] But, you know,
it's a bit better looking than Uncle. I shouldn't be surprised
if some people would think that Ape handsome.

HERBERT. Go on! You're getting depraved tastes, you are.
I shan't have nothing to do with you if you get struck on an
ape.

FLORRIE. You great silly! What's it matter when it's all
caged up? But if one of them creatures escaped on a dark
night, I bet you many a poor girl wouldn't hardly know the
difference.

HERBERT. I shan't take you to a Zoo again. It makes you
peculiar.

FLORRIE. You mean it makes you jealous!

HERBERT. Well, what if it does? Wouldn't any man feel
jealous if his fiancy suddenly admired an ape?

FLORRIE. You needn't worry. It's not a bit like you.

HERBERT. [*sulkily.*] I should just think it isn't. Nice thing
if you had to choose between an ape and me.

FLORRIE. Most girls have to.

HERBERT. Whatever *do* you mean?

FLORRIE. [*evasively.*] Oh, I don't know! [*Turning to him.*]
Anyway, I can't even admire a poor animal in a cage but you
get all upset. You were perfectly ridiculous over them
leopards.

HERBERT. And so were you! The next minute you'd have told me you wished I had spots!

FLORRIE. I didn't need to wish that. You've got 'em already.

HERBERT. That's right! Make a day of it!

FLORRIE. Only because you're so aggravating. You're a proper Mohammedan over women. You'd like to put veils under our noses and shut us up and pay unicorns to look after us, you would.

HERBERT. [*trying to take her hand.*] Can't you see it's because I'm so fond of you?

FLORRIE. Fond of me! You've queer ways of showing it, I must say!

HERBERT. But you know it's true. And as soon as Grandfather snuffs it and I get the shop, we'll settle down for good and all.

FLORRIE. And a nice life I'll have of it, married to an old Turk what won't let me even look out of the window!

HERBERT. I'll let you look out of the window, sure enough —and a better view you couldn't have: all down the Hotspur Road right up to the Rag and Bone Market.

FLORRIE. [*softening.*] It's a nice enough little place, I'll admit that.

HERBERT. [*ruminating, wistfully.*] Confectionery's so *refined*. And the best of it is, it's *absolutely* confectionery. It ain't even half fish or half tobacco. Ah, Florrie, you don't know how I ache for the time when we'll settle down. I can see us sitting in front of the fire on a winter's night, looking at each other, and then the bell tinkles and "Shop!" I says, and out you goes——

FLORRIE. Or out *you* goes!

HERBERT. Turn and turn about, of course. And then, in

the morning, when we're snug in bed and the alarm rings, I hits you, playful like, and "Awake, my soul!" I says, and up you gets——

FLORRIE. Oh, do I?

HERBERT. Or I do, of course—anyway, it'll all be lovely, and I shan't be jealous no more, because I shall have got you, good and fast, like as you'd been glued to me with secotine. . . .

FLORRIE. [suddenly.] Why does that thing rattle the bars of its cage?

HERBERT. Expect it's finished the bun it was eating and wants another. Greedy creatures, apes.

FLORRIE. Well, it can't have one, so that's that. [Leaning back.] Go on talking. It's kind of luxurious and Eastern-like with you telling me you loves me and that Ape listening, and all of them monkeys in the next room. It's what they call exotic.[1]

HERBERT. Well, I loves you so much that when I sees Grandfather toddling about with one foot in the grave, I feel like helping him to put the other foot in quick, and then we'll all be happy. You know, they settle these things much better where that Ape comes from. I once heard a missionary tell a beautiful story about how they make all the old 'uns climb a tree, and then they give the tree a good shake, and—who are you staring at?

FLORRIE. [hastily.] Only looking at the people going round, silly.

HERBERT. There ain't nobody going round. You were staring at that young man through there. [He points to L. entrance.] Do you know 'im?

FLORRIE. 'Course I don't. Won't you never stop worrying?

---

[1] Belonging to another part of the world, and therefore, strange.

And the more I think of it, the more I don't believe you loves me.

HERBERT. [*astonished.*] But I keep on telling you I do! You don't let me say nothing else. And I don't like the look of that young man. Well, now, they gives the tree a good shake, and——

FLORRIE. Then, if you loved me you'd go and buy a bun for that poor Ape.

HERBERT. Why, you said it couldn't 'ave one just now!

FLORRIE. Well, I've got a soft heart and changed my mind. [*She endeavors to conceal her interest in the room on the* L.]

HERBERT. And if you have, why should *I* go and get the bun?

FLORRIE. To please me, of course.

HERBERT. But I keep on pleasing you.

FLORRIE. [*turning to him.*] You seem mighty certain of that, always. How do you know you do?

HERBERT. Why, I took you to this Zoo, and at every cage I stopped and told you I loved you, just to keep your mind off the animals, and as soon as we sat down, I began again. What more do you want?

FLORRIE. I want you to go and get a bun when I ask you. [*With sarcasm.*] Must I give you the penny for it before you'll go?

HERBERT. [*rising, deeply hurt.*] Florrie! You needn't insinuate I don't know how to be the gentleman! I can behave on an outing, I can. You shall have your blasted bun—and I hope it chokes the brute!

[*He goes out with dignity through* R. *entrance.* FLORRIE *beckons violently to the* L. CLARENCE *appears at once in* L. *entrance.*]

CLARENCE. Florrie! You couldn't have done it better.

[*Coming quickly to the seat.*] Where's he gone?

FLORRIE. To get a bun for *that*. [*She points to the Ape.*]

CLARENCE. That? [*He sees the Ape.*] Oh, look at it! What's it do?

FLORRIE. Hops about in the background, like you.

CLARENCE. [*standing beside her,* L.] Sometimes I come to the foreground, don't you forget.

FLORRIE [*moving a little away from him to* R.] And don't you forget that if you're in the foreground when he comes back, there'll be such a row that we'll all be turned out.

CLARENCE. Then we'd better make the most of things now. [*Sitting down at* L. *end of seat and throwing his arms around her.*] Oh, Florrie, this is heaven!

FLORRIE. [*struggling as becomes her.*] O—o—o, Clarence! Suppose people saw us!

CLARENCE. I don't care. Neither should you. Love is beyond convention—you ask that Ape if it isn't. Besides, everyone's gone to see the lions fed. Tell me, Florrie, does he ever kiss you?

FLORRIE. *Him?* Lots and lots of times.

CLARENCE. Like this? [*Demonstration.*]

FLORRIE. Of course not. He couldn't if he tried.

CLARENCE. Then why do you take on with a poor spirited chap like that? Why don't you follow the promptings of your heart?

FLORRIE. You needn't make it difficult for me, Clarence. I'm in a funny mood to-day. Only just now I thought that Ape handsome.

CLARENCE. Well, three cheers for the Ape if it puts you in the correct disposition!

FLORRIE. [*gloomily.*] Don't you be so silly. You know very

well *you* can't support me in the luxury to which I've been accustomed. *You* haven't got no prospects.

CLARENCE. And has he?

FLORRIE. Rather! Why, he's all prospects and nothing else. High-class confectioner's shop in the Hotspur Road, it is. Sure thing as soon as his Grandfather hops it. I shall be a lady for life.

CLARENCE. I might have known it was something worldly and base.

FLORRIE. [*annoyed.*] Base yourself! Fancy asking me to come and look after you in them lodgings in Mersey Road!

CLARENCE. You see, I believe in true love. Forms and ceremonies ain't nothing to a true lover.

FLORRIE. A girl what turns down forms and ceremonies and goes in for true love deserves all she gets.

CLARENCE. And what happens to the worldly ones who sell their soul for gold and position? Oh, I know what it'll be like. There you'll sit, and suddenly the bell'll go and "Shop!" he'll holler——

FLORRIE. [*clinging to him.*] Oh, Clarence, don't for goodness' sake!

CLARENCE. [*rather surprised at his success.*] I—I thought it'd bring it home to you. But that's nothing. When he's in a bad mood he'll heave the confectionery at you until your own family can't identify you.

FLORRIE. [*letting him go.*] Clarence, just you stop tormenting. There's going to be no confectionery heaving if I know it; and I ain't the only woman whose had to choose between her career and her heart.

[*The Ape, who has been restlessly walking about, comes close to the bars of the cage and peers at them.*]

CLARENCE. [*seizing her hands.*] Your heart? Then you *do* love me, Florrie?

FLORRIE. Of course I do, because you can be real passionate—and I do love a bit of passion sometimes. But passion won't get me as far as Mersey Road.

CLARENCE. There ain't no *shop* in Mersey Road.

FLORRIE. There ain't nothing in Mersey Road except a bit of pawing about. Don't you let this Zoo give you false impressions. This is England, not Buenos Aires!

CLARENCE. Florrie, for the last time, will you sacrifice your heart and your deepest instincts for the sake of worldly gain? Won't you be like Marguerite and Helen of Troy and Cleopatra and come with me to Mersey Road?

FLORRIE. [*almost yielding.*] Clarence, you've that persuasive—— [*She turns her head and comes face to face with the Ape.*] O—o—o! [*Breaking away from him.*] No, I won't!

CLARENCE. [*furious.*] I thought you liked that Ape!

FLORRIE. It's taught me a lesson.

CLARENCE. Oh, has it? Well, you won't thank it for that lesson in a year's time!

FLORRIE. No, but I shall in twenty.

CLARENCE. [*throwing up her hands.*] It's hopeless! I give up the struggle. This is our last meeting, Florrie.

FLORRIE. Perhaps it'd better be—but I must say I never thought it would take place in front of an ape.

CLARENCE. A meddlesome and dangerous beast what ought to be destroyed.

FLORRIE. I thought you liked that Ape.

CLARENCE. Liked it? Didn't it come up and make a muck of everything?

FLORRIE. I shouldn't be surprised if that Ape's been put there especially to help me.

CLARENCE. That's blasphemy, that is. I bet it don't help you again.

FLORRIE. You never know—and, anyway, don't forget Herbert's coming back to give it a bun any minute.

CLARENCE. He's every reason to give it a hundred buns, blast him!

FLORRIE. [*moving nearer to him.*] Clarence, you're wasting precious moments, you are. But you always talked too much.

CLARENCE. You're right, Florrie. It ain't no good talking, leastways, not to you. It's all over, I can see that. Come and give me a long, long kiss for the last time. [*They fall into a tragic embrace.*]

FLORRIE. [*wiping away a tear.*] I shan't forget you, never.

CLARENCE. Oh yes, you will. You haven't even got a photograph to remember me by. You've always refused every one I've offered you.

FLORRIE. Well, I was frightened of Herbert finding it and asking silly questions.

CLARENCE. You see, you won't take *no* risks for me.

FLORRIE. I will. I'll take one now. If you've got a photograph, I'll have it.

CLARENCE. I've had one ready for you for a long time. Had it made into a locket, just to please you. See? [*He produces a rather ornate locket from his waistcoat pocket and displays it.*]

FLORRIE. [*taking it.*] Oh, Clarence, it's lovely. It's got just your look when you gave me them peppermints.

CLARENCE. [*working himself up.*] And will you gaze at it

on summer evenings when the shop's going badly and every-thing's melting, and think of the man you lost?

FLORRIE. [*wiping away some more tears.*] I will—but the shop ain't going to go badly, and there's an electric fan!

CLARENCE. [*moving close to her.*] And will you remember to your dying day the longing, lingering, loving kiss I'm going to give you now?

FLORRIE. You bet I will—— [*Looking quickly towards* R.] Oh, stop! He's coming back! 'Course he *would,* just when I was going to enjoy myself!

[*They break apart.*]

[*Enter* HERBERT, *through* R. *entrance, with a little paper bag in his hand.*]

[*To* CLARENCE—*with heavily assumed indifference.*] Well —so long! [*She pops the locket in her bag.*]

CLARENCE. [*also pulling himself together and rising.*] So long!

[*He endeavors to stroll off, jauntily whistling, through* L. *entrance.*]

HERBERT. [*when he has gone; with intensity.*] And who was that, may I ask? [*Stands by her,* R.]

FLORRIE. [*playing with her umbrella.*] Oh, just a young man.

HERBERT. Thank you. I can see that for myself. And the same young man you was staring at when you sent me on a fool's errand for a bun if I'm not mistaken! [*Endeavoring to look like Napoleon.*] Now, what's been going on?

FLORRIE. Nothing special.

HERBERT. Nothing special? Just look at your hat! Call that nothing special?

FLORRIE. [*hastily putting her hands to her hat.*] Whatever's the matter with my hat?

HERBERT. All knocked endways as vulgar as anything, and your face flushed up on one side. Nice goings on there's been in this Ape house, my word.

FLORRIE. Can't you see the Ape had at me?

HERBERT. If anything had at you it was that young man.

FLORRIE. Whose being vulgar now? I tell you, I was sitting here thinking of you, quiet like, when the Ape comes up, all ferocious, and tries to claw my hat and get at my blouse, and a young man who was passing was so good as to come and drive it off, and that's all about it. Why, you ought to have thanked him if you'd any manners.

HERBERT. Where's his manners, not stopping? He didn't wait for any thanks, did he? He was away pretty quick, wasn't he? Trying to whistle, unconcerned, too, to put me off. [*Examining the cage.*] It's a nice little tale you've told, but that Ape couldn't get anywhere near enough to knock you about; besides, I expect it was so horrified at what was going on it was rooted to the spot.

FLORRIE. [*holding her own.*] Call yourself a gentleman and insinuate such things! I tell you, a young fellow came and rescued me. Very nice he was about it, too.

HERBERT. He must have been, considering he gave you a present to remember him by.

FLORRIE. [*really startled.*] What do you mean?

HERBERT. [*triumphing.*] I saw you pop something into your bag as soon as I came in! I bet it was his photograph! Now, look here, Florrie, if I find another man's photograph in that bag, everything's a wash-out, I can tell you that.

FLORRIE. [*agitated.*] I don't know how you can imagine such things. Proper filthy mind, you've got.

HERBERT. I don't need to imagine. I bet your behavior's been a disgrace to a respectable Ape house! That's why he went off whistling like a damn canary, knowing all the time his silly face was in your bag ready for you to slobber over as soon as you got home. Regular passport-photo it'll be, too! Well, if you've been playing false to me while I was fetching a bun for your blasted Ape, the marriage arranged between Herbert Jones and Florrie Bently will not take place. Foreign and Colonial papers please copy. [*He strikes what he hopes is a terribly effective attitude.*]

FLORRIE. [*rallying.*] Well, I've never been so insulted before! Do you think for a moment that I'd go popping some other fellow's photograph in my bag when I was promised to you?

HERBERT. Well, you open it and let me see.

FLORRIE. [*at her wits' end.*] You mean to say you can't trust me.

HERBERT. No, I can't, and I'm not going to attempt the impossible. Open that bag.

FLORRIE. [*clinging tightly to the bag.*] I'll do nothing of the kind! [*Suddenly she looks at the Ape and is struck with an idea.*] Here, give me that bun!

HERBERT. [*amazed.*] Why on earth? If that Ape's been as fresh as you say, you'd never want to feed it! I know you. You'd be asking me to give it a lam on the head.

FLORRIE. [*snatching the paper bag from him.*] I wish you would give it a lam on the head, Herbert, I do really! After the way it frightened me, it deserves a clump. Here's my umbrella! If you can reach it, you shall have my bag to open.

HERBERT. [*taking the umbrella.*] Honest?

FLORRIE. Honest. Go and give it a good swipe before the Keeper catches you.

[*She tears open the paper bag and extracts the bun while* HERBERT, *umbrella in hand, stalks round* R. *to the cage.*]

HERBERT. [*his back turned to her and vainly trying to get at the Ape.*] I can't get near the darned thing! It's much more difficult than you'd think.

FLORRIE. [*opening her bag hastily, taking out locket and stuffing it inside the bun.*] Don't you be discouraged, Herbert. Try, try, try again.

HERBERT. [*exhausted.*] I—I believe I touched it then. It turned its head towards me.

FLORRIE. Well, that'll do. Now it can have the bun to soothe it down.

HERBERT. [*coming round* R. *to seat.*] Changed your mind and gone soft-hearted again, I suppose?

FLORRIE. Of course! You don't know what a nice nature I've got. Here, [*getting up and going to the Ape*] come along! Have a bun. I forgive you, I do. [*The Ape snatches at the bun.*]

HERBERT. Well, it's got the bun and now I'll have the bag.

FLORRIE. [*watching with great anxiety.*] Wait—wait until it's swallowed it. [*The Ape gulps down the bun.* FLORRIE *comes quickly to the front.*] Now! [*She faces him with scorn.*] Take the bag and open it, you unbelieving, ungrateful, suspicious, mean, jealous, miserable creature! Take the bag, open it; have a look at the lip-stick, powder your nose with the compact, mix up the Asperos with the nail-polish, break the looking-glass, count the coppers, do, and help yourself, but don't you never dare to doubt a woman's word again! There!

[*She showers the contents of the bag over him—pennies roll in all directions.* HERBERT *drops the umbrella.*]

Have a look at everything, don't miss nothing—it might keep you awake if you missed something! [*Throwing the bag in his face.*] Tear the bag to pieces, I don't mind! I'd rather lose everything I possessed than have my honor doubted. Everything's a wash-out, is it? It'd better be if you haven't the common decency to trust your future wife!

HERBERT. [*overwhelmed, and trying to pick up the contents of the bag.*] I'm sure I beg your pardon, Florrie, I really do. I expect I've been a bit mean. I never thought you'd take it like this! Never!

FLORRIE. [*enjoying herself.*] And what way was I to take it, I'd like to know? A poor girl is rescued from the jaws of an infuriated animal and has to put up with third degree from her fiancy in consequence. I'm not only sticking up for myself. I'm sticking up for womanhood all over the world, I am. Just you remember that a woman's word is sacred, and don't you never dare to doubt it again!

HERBERT. I won't, Florrie, I won't. I feel real humbled. [*Tries to pick up coppers, etc.*]

FLORRIE. *And* when we're sitting together on quiet winter evenings and the bell tinkles and I says "Shop!"—who goes out?

HERBERT. [*endeavoring to pick up various articles.*] I do, Florrie, I assure you!

FLORRIE. *And* when we're snug in bed in the morning and the alarm rings, who hits who playful like, and says, "Awake, my soul"?

HERBERT [*still busy.*] I do, Florrie, without a doubt.

FLORRIE. And what happens then?

HERBERT. I gets up and brings you a cup of tea! [*Getting up with his arms full.*] Oh, won't you give me a kiss, just to show forgiveness?

FLORRIE. [*taking umbrella, bag, etc., from him and stuffing things in the bag.*] *Forgiveness?* There ain't going to be no forgiveness until I've had one of them cups of tea now.

HERBERT. All right, I'll take you to the cafe; but just before we go I'd like a kiss to show—O—o! Look at the Ape!

FLORRIE. What on earth's the matter with it now?

HERBERT. It's got its hand on its stomach and has gone all grey—I'm sure it's going to be sick!

FLORRIE. [*terrified, and seizing* HERBERT's *hand.*] Come along home at once!

HERBERT. Why, whatever's the hurry?

FLORRIE. [*with determination.*] Never you mind. You come along NOW!

CURTAIN

IN THE ZONE

by

EUGENE O'NEILL

Out of his early experiences as able seaman our foremost dramatist, Eugene O'Neill wrote a number of short sea plays which were later published under the title of *S.S. Glencairn*. The one-act play here included paints rough and vivid characters found aboard a British ship passing through submarine-infested waters during World War I. The language is pungent and pointed.

Eugene O'Neill, son of a celebrated actor, has lived through trying experiences, has mastered the art of playwriting, experimented with many styles, and won the Pulitzer Prize three times. In addition, the highest international honor, The Nobel Prize for Literature, was awarded him in 1936. Since then other honors have been showered upon him.

Many of his longer plays have been highly praised and produced in countries aboard.

EUGENE O'NEILL
AMERICA'S FOREMOST DRAMATIST.

IN THE ZONE

CHARACTERS

SMITTY	PAUL
DAVIS	JACK
SWANSON	DRISCOLL
SCOTTY	COCKY
IVAN	

Seamen on the British Tramp Steamer
  "Glencairn."

SCENE: *The seamen's forecastle. On the right above the bunks three or four portholes covered with black cloth can be seen. On the floor near the doorway is a pail with a tin dipper. A lantern in the middle of the floor, turned down very low, throws a dim light around the place. Five men,* SCOTTY, IVAN, SWANSON, SMITTY *and* PAUL, *are in their bunks apparently asleep. It is about ten minutes of twelve on a night in the fall of the year 1915.*

SMITTY *turns slowly in his bunk and, leaning out over the side, looks from one to another of the men as if to assure himself that they are asleep. Then he climbs carefully out of his bunk and stands in the middle of the forecastle fully dressed, but in his stocking feet, glancing around him suspiciously. Reassured, he leans down and cautiously pulls out a suit-case from under the bunks in front of him.*

Just at this moment DAVIS *appears in the doorway, carrying a large steaming coffee-pot in his hand. He stops short when he sees* SMITTY. *A puzzled expression comes over his face, followed by one of suspicion, and he retreats farther back in the alleyway, where he can watch* SMITTY *without being seen.*

All the latter's movements indicate a fear of discovery. He takes out a small bunch of keys and unlocks the suit-case, making a slight noise as he does so. SCOTTY *wakes up and peers at him over the side of the bunk.* SMITTY *opens the suit-case and takes out a small black tin box, carefully places this under his mattress, shoves the suit-case back under the bunk, climbs into his bunk again, closes his eyes and begins to snore loudly.*

DAVIS *enters the forecastle, places the coffee-pot beside the lantern, and goes from one to the other of the sleepers and shakes them vigorously, saying to each in a low voice: "Near eight bells, Scotty. Arise and shine, Swanson. Eight bells, Ivan."* SMITTY *yawns loudly with a great pretense of having been dead asleep. All of the rest of the men tumble out of their bunks, stretching and gaping, and commence to pull on their shoes. They go one by one to the cupboard near the open door, take out their cups and spoons, and sit down together on the benches. The coffee-pot is passed around. They munch their biscuits and sip their coffee in dull silence.*

DAVIS. [*suddenly jumping to his feet—nervously.*] Where's that air comin' from? [*All are startled and look at him wonderingly.*]

SWANSON. [*a squat, surly-faced Swede—grumpily.*] What air? I don't feel nothing.

DAVIS. [*excitedly.*] I kin feel it—a draft. [*He stands on the bench and looks around—suddenly exploding.*] Damn fool square-head! [*He leans over the upper bunk in which* PAUL *is sleeping and slams the porthole shut.*] I got a good notion to report him. Serve him bloody well right! What's the use o' blindin' the ports when that thick-head goes an' leaves 'em open?

SWANSON. [*yawning—too sleepy to be aroused by anything—carelessly.*] Dey don't see what little light go out yust one port.

SCOTTY. [*protestingly.*] Dinna be a loon, Swanson! D'ye no ken the dangerr o' showin' a licht wi' a pack o' submarrines lyin' aboot?

IVAN. [*shaking his shaggy ox-like head in an emphatic affirmative.*] Dot's right, Scotty. I don' li-ike blow up, no, by devil!

SMITTY. [*his manner slightly contemptuous.*] I don't think there's much danger of meeting any of their submarines, not until we get into the War Zone, at any rate.

DAVIS. [*he and* SCOTTY *look at* SMITTY *suspiciously—harshly.*] You don't, eh? [*He lowers his voice and speaks slowly.*] Well, we're in the war zone right this minit if you wants to know. [*The effect of this speech is instantaneous. All sit bolt upright on their benches and stare at* DAVIS.]

SMITTY. How do you know, Davis?

DAVIS. [*angrily.*] 'Cos Drisc heard the First send the Third below to wake the skipper when we fetched the zone—bout five bells, it was. Now whata y' got to say?

SMITTY. [*conciliatingly.*] Oh, I wasn't doubting your word, Davis; but you know they're not pasting up bulletins to let the crew know when the zone is reached—especially on ammunition ships like this.

IVAN. [*decidedly.*] I don't li-ike dees voyage. Next time I ship on windjammer Boston to River Plate, load with wood only so it float, by golly!

SWANSON. [*fretfully.*] I hope British navy blow 'em to hell, those submarines, py damn!

SCOTTY. [*looking at* SMITTY, *who is staring at the doorway in a dream, his chin on his hands. Meaningly.*] It is no the submarrines only we've to fear, I'm thinkin'.

DAVIS. [*assenting eagerly.*] That's no lie, Scotty.

SWANSON. You mean the mines?

SCOTTY. I wasna thinkin' o' mines eitherr.

DAVIS. There's many a good ship blown up and at the bottom of the sea, what never hit no mine or torpedo.

SCOTTY. Did ye neverr read of the German spies and the dirrty work they're doin' all the war? [*He and* DAVIS *both glance at* SMITTY, *who is deep in thought and is not listening to the conversation.*]

DAVIS. An' the clever way they fool you!

SWANSON. Sure! I read it in paper many time.

DAVIS. Well—[*He is about to speak but hesitates and finishes lamely.*]—you got to watch out, that's all I says.

IVAN. [*drinking the last of his coffee and slamming his fist on the bench explosively.*] I tell you dis rotten coffee give me belly-ache, yes! [*They all look at him in amused disgust.*]

SCOTTY. [*sardonically.*] Dinna fret about it, Ivan. If we blow up ye'll no be mindin' the pain in your middle.

[JACK *enters. He is a young American with a tough, good-natured face. He wears dungarees and a heavy jersey.*]

JACK. Eight bells, fellers.

IVAN. [*stupidly.*] I don' hear bell ring.

JACK. No, and yuh won't hear any ring, yuh boob—[*Lowering his voice unconsciously.*]—now we're in the war zone.

SWANSON. [*anxiously.*] Is the boats all ready?

JACK. Sure; we can lower 'em in a second.

DAVIS. A lot o' good the boats'll do, with us loaded deep with all kinds o' dynamite and stuff the like o' that! If a torpedo hits this hooker we'll all be in hell b'fore you could wink your eye.

JACK. They ain't goin' to hit us, see? That's my dope. Whose wheel is it?

IVAN. [*sullenly.*] My wheel. [*He lumbers out.*]

JACK. And whose lookout?

SWANSON. Mine, I tink. [*He follows* IVAN.]

JACK. [*scornfully.*] A hell of a lot of use keepin' a lookout! We couldn't run away or fight if we wanted to. [*To* SCOTTY *and* SMITTY.] Better look up the bo'sun or the Fourth, you two, and let 'em see you're awake. [SCOTTY *goes to the doorway and turns to wait for* SMITTY, *who is still in the same position, head on hands, seemingly unconscious of everything.* JACK *slaps him roughly on the shoulder and he comes to with a start.*] Aft and report, Duke! What's the matter with yuh— in a dope dream? [SMITTY *goes out after* SCOTTY *without answering.* JACK *looks after him with a frown.*] He's a queer guy. I can't figger him out.

DAVIS. Nor no one else. [*Lowering his voice—meaningly.*] An' he's liable to turn out queerer than any of us think if we ain't careful.

JACK. [*suspiciously.*] What d'yuh mean? [*They are interrupted by the entrance of* DRISCOLL *and* COCKY.]

COCKY. [*protestingly.*] Blimey if I don't fink I'll put in this 'ere watch ahtside on deck. [*He and* DRISCOLL *go over and get their cups.*] I down't want to be caught in this 'ole if they 'its us. [*He pours out coffee.*]

DRISCOLL. [*pouring his.*] Divil a bit ut wud matther where ye arre. Ye'd be blown to smithereens b'fore ye cud say your name. [*He sits down, over-turning as he does so the untouched cup of coffee which* SMITTY *had forgotten and left on the bench. They all jump nervously as the tin cup hits the floor with a bang.* DRISCOLL *flies into an unreasoning rage.*] Who's the dirty scut left this cup where a man 'ud sit on ut?

DAVIS. It's Smitty's.

DRISCOLL. [*kicking the cup across the forecastle.*] Does he think he's too much av a bloody gentleman to put his own away loike the rist av us? If he does I'm the bye'll beat that noshun out av his head.

COCKY. Be the airs 'e puts on you'd think 'e was the Prince of Wales. Wot's 'e doin' on a ship, I arsks yer? 'E ain't now good as a sailor, is 'e?—dawdlin' abaht on deck like a chicken wiv 'is 'ead cut orf!

JACK. [*good-naturedly.*] Aw, the Duke's all right. S'posin' he did ferget his cup—what's the dif! [*He picks up the cup and puts it away—with a grin.*] This war zone stuff's got yer goat, Drisc—and yours too, Cocky—and I ain't cheerin' much fur it myself, neither.

COCKY. [*with a sigh.*] Blimey, it ain't no bleedin' joke, yer first trip, to know as ther's a ship full of shells li'ble to go orf in under your bloomin' feet, as you might say, if we gets 'it be a torpedo or mine. [*With sudden savagery.*] Calls they-selves 'uman bein's, too! Blarsted 'Uns!

DRISCOLL. [*gloomily.*] 'Tis me last trip in the bloody zone, God help me. The divil take their twenty-foive percent bonus—and be drowned like a rat in a trap in the bargain, maybe.

DAVIS. Wouldn't be so bad if she wasn't carryin' ammunition. Them's the kind the subs is layin' for.

DRISCOLL. [*irritably.*] Fur the love av hivin', don't be talkin' about ut. I'm sick wid thinkin' and jumpin' at iviry bit av a noise. [*There is a pause during which they all stare gloomily at the floor.*]

JACK. Hey, Davis, what was you sayin' about Smitty when they came in?

DAVIS. [*with a great air of mystery.*] I'll tell you in a minit.

I want to wait an' see if he's comin' back. [*Impressively.*] You won't be callin' him all right when you hears what I seen with my own eyes. [*He adds with an air of satisfaction.*] An' you won't be feelin' no safer, neither. [*They all look at him with puzzled glances full of a vague apprehension.*]

DRISCOLL. God blarst ut! [*He fills his pipe and lights it. The others, with an air of remembering something they had forgotten, do the same.* SCOTTY *enters.*]

SCOTTY. [*in awed tones.*] Mon, but it's clear outside the nicht! Like day.

DAVIS. [*in low tones.*] Where's Smitty, Scotty?

SCOTTY. Out on the hatch starin' at the moon like a mon half-daft.

DAVIS. Kin you see him from the doorway?

SCOTTY. [*goes to doorway and carefully peeks out.*] Aye; he's still there.

DAVIS. Keep your eyes on him for a moment. I've got something I wants to tell the boys and I don't want him walkin' in the middle of it. Give a shout if he starts this way.

SCOTTY. [*with suppressed excitement.*] Aye, I'll watch him. And I've somethin' myself to tell aboot his Lordship.

DRISCOLL. [*impatiently.*] Out wid ut! You're talkin' more than a pair av auld women wud be standin' in the road, and gettin' no further along.

DAVIS. Listen! You 'member when I went to git the coffee, Jack?

JACK. Sure, I do.

DAVIS. Well, I brings it down here same as usual and got as far as the door there when I sees him.

JACK. Smitty?

DAVIS. Yes, Smitty! He was standin' in the middle of the fo'c'stle there [*Pointing.*] lookin' around sneakin'like at Ivan and Swanson and the rest's if he wants to make certain they're asleep. [*He pauses significantly, looking from one to the other of his listeners.* SCOTTY *is nervously dividing his attention between* SMITTY *on the hatch outside and* DAVIS' *story, fairly bursting to break in with his own revelations.*]

JACK. [*impatiently.*] What of it?

DAVIS. Listen! He was standin' right there—[*Pointing again.*]—in his stockin' feet—no shoes on, mind, so he wouldn't make no noise!

JACK. [*spitting disgustedly.*] Aw!

DAVIS. [*not heeding the interruption.*] I seen right away somethin' on the queer was up so I slides back into the alleyway where I kin see him but he can't see me. After he makes sure they're all asleep he goes in under the bunks there—bein' careful not to raise a noise, mind!—an' takes out his bag there. [*By this time every one,* JACK *included, is listening breathlessly to his story.*] Then he fishes in his pocket an' takes out a bunch o' keys an' kneels down beside the bag an' opens it.

SCOTTY. [*unable to keep silent longer.*] Mon, didn't I see him do that same thing wi' these two eyes. 'Twas just that moment I woke and spied him.

DAVIS. [*surprised, and a bit nettled to have to share his story with any one.*] Oh, you seen him, too, eh? [*To the others.*] Then Scotty kin tell you if I'm lyin' or not.

DRISCOLL. An' what did he do whin he'd the bag opened?

DAVIS. He bends down and reaches out his hand sort o' scared-like, like it was somethin' dang'rous he was after, an' feels round in under his duds—hidden in under his duds an' wrapped up in 'em, it was—an' he brings out a black iron box!

COCKY. [*looking around him with a frightened glance.*] Gawd blimey! [*The others likewise betray their uneasiness, shuffling their feet nervously.*]

DAVIS. Ain't that right, Scotty?

SCOTTY. Right as rain, I'm tellin' ye!

DAVIS. [*to the others with an air of satisfaction.*] There you are! [*Lowering his voice.*] An' then what d'you suppose he did? Sneaks to his bunk an' slips the black box in under his mattress—in under his mattress, mind!

JACK. And it's there now?

DAVIS. 'Course it is! [JACK *starts toward* SMITTY's *bunk.* DRISCOLL *grabs him by the arm.*]

DRISCOLL. Don't be touchin' ut, Jack!

JACK. Yuh needn't worry. I ain't goin' to touch it. [*He pulls up* SMITTY's *mattress and looks down. The others stare at him, holding their breaths. He turns to them, trying hard to assume a careless tone.*] It's there, aw right.

COCKY. [*miserably upset.*] I'm gointer 'op it aht on deck. [*He gets up but* DRISCOLL *pulls him down again.* COCKY *protests.*] It fair guvs me the trembles sittin' still in 'ere.

DRISCOLL. [*scornfully.*] Are ye frightened, ye toad? 'Tis a hell av a thing fur grown men to be shiverin' loike childer at a bit av a black box. [*Scratching his head in uneasy perplexity.*] Still, ut's damn queer, the looks av ut.

DAVIS. [*sacrastically.*] A bit of a black box, eh? How big d'you think them—[*He hesitates.*]—things has to be—big as this fo'c'stle?

JACK. [*in a voice meant to be reassuring.*] Aw, hell! I'll bet it ain't nothin' but some coin he's saved he's got locked up in there.

DAVIS. [*scornfully.*] That's likely, ain't it? Then why does he act so 'spicious? He's been on ship near two year, ain't he? He knows damn well there ain't no thiefs in this fo'c'stle, don't he? An' you know's well's I do he didn't have no money when he came on board an' he ain't saved none since.

Don't you? [JACK *doesn't answer.*] Listen! D'you know what he done after he put that thing in under his mattress?—an' Scotty'll tell you if I ain't speakin' truth. He looks round to see if any one's woke up——

SCOTTY. I clapped my eyes shut when he turned round.

DAVIS. An' then he crawls into his bunk an' shuts his eyes, an' starts in *snorin', pretending* he was asleep, mind!

SCOTTY. Aye, I could hear him.

DAVIS. An' when I goes to call him I don't even shake him. I just says, "Eight bells, Smitty," in a'most a whisperlike, an' up he gets yawnin' an' stretchin' fit to kill hisself 's if he'd been dead asleep.

COCKY. Gawd blimey!

DRISCOLL. [*shaking his head.*] Ut looks bad, divil a doubt av ut.

DAVIS. [*excitedly.*] An' now I come to think of it, there's the porthole. How'd it come to git open, tell me that? I know'd well Paul never opened it. Ain't he grumblin' about bein' cold all the time?

SCOTTY. The mon that opened it meant no good to this ship, whoever he was.

JACK. [*sourly.*] What porthole? What're yuh talkin' about?

DAVIS. [*pointing over* PAUL's *bunk.*] There. It was open when I come in. I felt the cold air on my neck an' shut it. It would'a been clear's a lighthouse to any sub that was watchin'—an' we s'posed to have all the ports blinded! Who'd do a dirty trick like that? It wasn't none of us, nor Scotty here, nor Swanson, nor Ivan. Who would it be, then?

COCKY. [*angrily.*] Must'a been 'is bloody Lordship.

DAVIS. For all's we know he might'a been signallin' with it. They does it like that by winkin' a light. Ain't you read how they gets caught doin' it in London an' on the coast?

COCKY. [*firmly convinced now.*] An' wot's 'e doin' aht alone on the 'atch—keepin' 'isself clear of us like 'e was afraid?

DRISCOLL. Kape your eye on him, Scotty.

SCOTTY. There's no a move oot o' him.

JACK. [*in irritated perplexity.*] But, hell, ain't he an Englishman? What'd he wanta——

DAVIS. English? How d'we know he's English? Cos he talks it? That ain't no proof. Ain't you read in the papers how all them German spies they been catchin' in England has been livin' there for ten, often as not twenty years, an' talks English as good 's any one? An' look here, ain't you noticed he don't talk natural? He talks it too damn good, that's what I mean. He don't talk exactly like a toff[1], does he, Cocky?

COCKY. Not like any toff as I ever met up wiv.

DAVIS. No; an' he don't talk it like us, that's certain. An' he don't look English. An' what d'we know about him when you come to look at it? Nothin'! He ain't ever said where he comes from or why. All we knows is he ships on here in London 'bout a year b'fore the war starts, as an A. B.—stole his papers most lik'ly—when he don't know how to box the compass, hardly. Ain't that queer in itself? An' was he ever open with us like a good shipmate? No; he's always had that sly air about him 's if he was hidin' somethin'.

DRISCOLL. [*slapping his thigh—angrily.*] Divil take me if I don't think ye have the truth av ut, Davis.

COCKY. [*scornfully.*] Lettin' on be 'is silly airs, and all, 'e's the son of a blarsted earl or somethink!

---

[1] A man who shows off his dress or manners.

DAVIS. An' the name he calls hisself—Smith! I'd risk a quid[2] of my next pay day that his real name is Schmidt, if the truth was known.

JACK. [*evidently fighting against his own conviction.*] Aw, say, you guys give me a pain! What'd they want puttin' a spy on this old tub for?

DAVIS. [*shaking his head sagely.*] They're deep ones, an' there's a lot o' things a sailor'll see in the ports he puts in ought to be useful to 'em. An' if he kin signal to 'em an' they blow us up it's one ship less, ain't it? [*Lowering his voice and indicating* SMITTY's *bunk.*] Or if he blows us up hisself.

SCOTTY. [*in alarmed tones.*] Hush, mon! Here he comes! [SCOTTY *hurries over to a bench and sits down. A thick silence settles over the forecastle. The men look from one to another with uneasy glances.* SMITTY *enters and sits down beside his bunk. He is seemingly unaware of the dark glances of suspicion directed at him from all sides. He slides his hand back stealthily over his mattress and his fingers move, evidently feeling to make sure the box is still there. The others follow this movement carefully with quick looks out of the corners of their eyes. Their attitudes grow tense as if they were about to spring at him. Satisfied the box is safe,* SMITTY *draws his hand away slowly and utters a sigh of relief.*]

SMITTY. [*in a casual tone which to them sounds sinister.*] It's a good light night for the subs if there's any about. [*For a moment he sits staring in front of him. Finally he seems to sense the hostile atmosphere of the forecastle and looks from one to the other of the men in surprise. All of them avoid his eyes. He sighs with a puzzled expression and gets up and walks out of the doorway. There is silence for a moment after his departure and then a storm of excited talk breaks loose.*]

[2] A one-pound note.

DAVIS. Did you see him feelin' if it was there?

COCKY. 'E ain't arf a sly one wiv 'is talk of submarines, Gawd blind 'im!

SCOTTY. Did ye see the sneakin' looks he gave us?

DRISCOLL. If ivir I saw black shame on a man's face 'twas on his whin he sat there!

JACK. [*thoroughly convinced at last.*] He looked bad to me. He's a crook, aw right.

DAVIS. [*excitedly.*] What'll we do? We gotter do some-thin' quick or—— [*He is interrupted by the sound of something hitting against the port side of the forecastle with a dull, heavy thud. The men start to their feet in wild-eyed terror and turn as if they were going to rush for the deck. They stand that way for a strained moment, scarcely breath-ing and listening intently.*]

JACK. [*with a sickly smile.*] Hell! It's on'y a piece of drift-wood or a floatin' log. [*He sits down again.*]

DAVIS. [*sarcastically.*] Or a mine that didn't go off—that time—or a piece o' wreckage from some ship they've sent to Davy Jones.

COCKY. [*mopping his brow with a trembling hand.*] Blimey! [*He sinks back weakly on a bench.*]

DRISCOLL. [*furiously.*] God blarst ut! No man at all cud be puttin' up wid the loike av this—an' I'm not wan to be fearin' anything or any man in the worrld'll stand up to me face to face; but this divil's trickery in the darrk—— [*He starts for* SMITTY's *bunk.*] I'll throw ut out wan av the port-holes an' be done wid ut. [*He reaches toward the mattress.*]

SCOTTY. [*grabbing his arm—wildly.*] Arre ye daft, mon?

DAVIS. Don't monkey with it, Drisc. I knows what to do. Bring the bucket o' water here, Jack, will you? [JACK *gets it and brings it over to* DAVIS.] An' you, Scotty, see if he's back on the hatch.

scotty. [*cautiously peering out.*] Aye, he's sittin' there the noo.

davis. Sing out if he makes a move. Lift up the mattress, Drisc—careful now! [driscoll *does so with infinite caution.*] Take it out, Jack—careful—don't shake it now, for Christ's sake! Here—put it in the water—easy! There, that's fixed it! [*They all sit down with great sighs of relief.*] The water'll git in and spoil it.

driscoll. [*slapping* davis *on the back.*] Good wurrk for ye, Davis, ye scut! [*He spits on his hands aggressively.*] An' now what's to be done wid that black-hearted thraitor?

cocky. [*belligerently.*] Guv 'im a shove in the marf and 'eave 'im over the side!

davis. An' serve him right!

jack. Aw, say, give him a chance. Yuh can't prove nothin' till yuh find out what's in there.

driscoll. [*heatedly.*] Is ut more proof ye'd be needin' afther what we've seen an' heard? Then listen to me—an' ut's Driscoll talkin'—if there's divilmint in that box an' we see plain 'twas his plan to murrdher his òwn shipmates that have served him fair—[*He raises his fist.*] I'll choke his rotten hearrt out wid me own hands, an' over the side wid him, and one man missin' in the mornin'.

davis. An' no one the wiser. He's the balmy kind what commits suicide.

cocky. They 'angs spies ashore.

jack. [*resentfully.*] If he's done what yuh think I'll croak him myself. Is that good enough for yuh?

driscoll. [*looking down at the box.*] How'll we be openin' this, I wonder?

scotty. [*from the doorway—warningly.*] He's standin' up.

davis. We'll take his keys away from him when he comes

in. Quick, Drisc! You an' Jack get beside the door and grab him. [*They get on either side of the door.* DAVIS *snatches a small coil of rope from one of the upper bunks.*] This'll do for me an' Scotty to tie him.

SCOTTY. He's turrnin' this way—he's comin'! [*He moves away from door.*]

DAVIS. Stand by to lend a hand, Cocky.

COCKY. Righto. [*As* SMITTY *enters the forecastle he is seized roughly from both sides and his arms pinned behind him. At first he struggles fiercely, but seeing the uselessness of this, he finally stands calmly and allows* DAVIS *and* SCOTTY *to tie up his arms.*]

SMITTY. [*when they have finished—with cold contempt.*] If this is your idea of a joke I'll have to confess it's a bit too thick for me to enjoy.

COCKY. [*angrily.*] Shut yer marf, 'ear!

DRISCOLL. [*roughly.*] Ye'll find ut's no joke, me bucko, b'fore we're done wid you. [*To* SCOTTY.] Kape your eye peeled, Scotty, and sing out if any one's comin'. [SCOTTY *resumes his post at the door.*]

SMITTY. [*with the same icy contempt.*] If you'd be good enough to explain——

DRISCOLL. [*furiously.*] Explain, is ut? 'Tis you'll do the explainin'—an' damn quick, or we'll know the reason why. [*To* JACK *and* DAVIS.] Bring him here, now. [*They push* SMITTY *over to the bucket.*] Look here, ye murrdherin' swab. D'you see ut? [SMITTY *looks down with an expression of amazement which rapidly changes to one of anguish.*]

DAVIS. [*with a sneer.*] Look at him! S'prised, ain't you? If you wants to try your dirty spyin' tricks on us you've gotter git up earlier in the mornin'.

COCKY. Thorght yer weren't 'arf a fox, didn't yer?

SMITTY. [*trying to restrain his growing rage.*] What—
what do you mean? That's only—— How dare—— What
are you doing with my private belongings?

COCKY. [*sarcastically.*] Ho yus! Private b'longings!

DRISCOLL. [*shouting.*] What is ut, ye swine? Will you tell
us to our faces? What's in ut?

SMITTY. [*biting his lips—holding himself in check with a
great effort.*] Nothing but—— That's my business. You'll
please attend to your own.

DRISCOLL. Oho, ut is, is ut? [*shaking his fist in* SMITTY's
face.] Talk aisy now if ye know what's best for you. Your
business, indade! Then we'll be makin' ut ours, I'm thinkin'.
[*To* JACK *and* DAVIS.] Take his keys away from him an' we'll
see if there's one'll open ut, maybe. [*They start in searching*
SMITTY, *who tries to resist and kicks out at the bucket.*
DRISCOLL *leaps forward and helps them push him away.*]
Try to kick ut over, wud ye? Did ye see him then?
Tryin' to murrdher us all, the scut! Take that pail out av his
way, Cocky.

[SMITTY *struggles with all of his strength and keeps them
busy for a few seconds. As* COCKY *grabs the pail* SMITTY
*makes a final effort and, lunging forward, kicks again at the
bucket but only succeeds in hitting* COCKY *on the shin.* COCKY
*immediately sets down the pail with a bang and, clutching
his knee in both hands, starts hopping around the forecastle,
groaning and swearing.*]

COCKY. Ooow! Gawd strike me pink! Kicked me, 'e did!
Bloody, bleedin', rotten Dutch 'og! [*Approaching* SMITTY,
*who has given up the fight and is pushed back against the
wall near the doorway with* JACK *and* DAVIS *holding him on
either side—wrathfully, at the top of his lungs.*] Kick me,
will yer? I'll show yer what for, yer bleedin' sneak! [*He
draws back his fist.* DRISCOLL *pushes him to one side.*]

DRISCOLL. Shut your mouth! D'you want to wake the whole ship? [COCKY *grumbles and retires to a bench, nursing his sore shin.*]

JACK. [*taking a small bunch of keys from* SMITTY'S *pocket.*] Here yuh are, Drisc.

DRISCOLL. [*taking them.*] We'll soon be knowin'. [*He takes the pail and sits down, placing it on the floor between his feet.* SMITTY *again tries to break loose but he is too tired and is easily held back against the wall.*]

SMITTY. [*breathing heavily and very pale.*] Cowards!

JACK. [*with a growl.*] Nix on the rough talk, see! That don't git yuh nothin'.

DRISCOLL. [*looking at the lock on the box in the water and then scrutinizing the keys in his hand.*] This'll be ut, I'm thinkin'. [*He selects one and gingerly reaches his hand in the water.*]

SMITTY. [*his face grown livid—chokingly.*] Don't you open that box, Driscoll. If you do, so help me God, I'll kill you if I have to hang for it.

DRISCOLL. [*pausing—his hand in the water.*] Whin I open this box I'll not be the wan to be kilt, me sonny bye! I'm no dirty spy.

SMITTY. [*his voice trembling with rage. His eyes are fixed on* DRISCOLL'S *hand.*] Spy? What are you talking about? I only put that box there so I could get it quick in case we were torpedoed. Are you all mad? Do you think I'm—— [*Chokingly.*] You stupid curs! You cowardly dolts! [DAVIS *claps his hand over* SMITTY'S *mouth.*]

DAVIS. That'll be enough from you! [DRISCOLL *takes the dripping box from the water and starts to fit in the key.* SMITTY *springs forward furiously, almost escaping from their grasp, and drags them after him half-way across the forecastle.*]

DRISCOLL. Hold him, ye divils! [*He puts the box back in the water and jumps to their aid.* COCKY *hovers on the outskirts of the battle, mindful of the kick he received.*]

SMITTY. [*raging.*] Cowards! Damn you! Rotten curs! [*He is thrown to the floor and held there.*] Cowards! Cowards!

DRISCOLL. I'll shut your dirty mouth for you. [*He goes to his bunk and pulls out a big wad of waste and comes back to* SMITTY.]

SMITTY. Cowards! Cowards!

DRISCOLL. [*with no gentle hand slaps the waste over* SMITTY's *mouth.*] That'll teach you to be misnamin' a man, ye sneak. Have ye a handkerchief, Jack? [JACK *hands him one and he ties it tightly around* SMITTY's *head over the waste.*] That'll fix your gab. Stand him up, now, and tie his feet, too, so he'll not be movin'. [*They do so and leave him with his back against the wall near* SCOTTY. *Then they all sit down beside* DRISCOLL, *who again lifts the box out of the water and sets it carefully on his knees. He picks out the key, then hesitates, looking from one to the other uncertainly.*] We'd best be takin' this to the skipper, d'you think, maybe?

JACK. [*irritably.*] To hell with the Old Man. This is our game and we c'n play it without no help.

COCKY. Now bleedin' horficers, I says!

DAVIS. They'd only be takin' all the credit and makin' heroes of theyselves.

DRISCOLL. [*boldly.*] Here goes, thin! [*He slowly turns the key in the lock. The others instinctively turn away. He carefully pushes the cover back on its hinges and looks at what he sees inside with an expression of puzzled astonishment. The others crowd up close. Even* SCOTTY *leaves his post to take a look.*] What is ut, Davis?

DAVIS. [*mystified.*] Looks funny, don't it? Somethin' square tied up in a rubber bag. Maybe it's dynamite—or somethin'—you can't never tell.

JACK. Aw, it ain't got no works so it ain't no bomb, I'll bet.

DAVIS. [*dubiously.*] They makes them all kinds, they do.

JACK. Open it up, Drisc.

DAVIS. Careful now! [DRISCOLL *takes a black rubber bag resembling a large tobacco pouch from the box and unties the string which is wound tightly around the top. He opens it and takes out a small packet of letters also tied up with string. He turns these over in his hands and looks at the others questioningly.*]

JACK. [*with a broad grin.*] On'y letters! [*Slapping* DAVIS *on the back.*] Yuh're a hell of a Sherlock Holmes, ain't yuh? Letters from his best girl too, I'll bet. Let's turn the Duke loose, what d'yuh say? [*He starts to get up.*]

DAVIS. [*fixing him with a withering look.*] Don't be so damn smart, Jack. Letters, you says, 's if there never was no harm in 'em. How d'you s'pose spies gets their orders and sends back what they finds out if it ain't by letters and such things? There's many a letter is worser'n any bomb.

COCKY. Righto! They ain't as innercent as they looks, I'll take me oath, when you read 'em. [*Pointing at* SMITTY.] Not 'is Lordship's letter; not be no means!

JACK. [*sitting down again.*] Well, read 'em and find out. [DRISCOLL *commences untying the packet. There is a muffled groan of rage and protest from* SMITTY.]

DAVIS. [*triumphantly.*] There! Listen to him! Look at him tryin' to get loose! Ain't that proof enough? He knows well we're findin' him out. Listen to me! Love letters, you says, Jack, 's if they couldn't harm nothin'. Listen! I was reading in some magazine in New York on'y two weeks back

how some German spy in Paris was writin' love letters to
some woman spy in Switzerland who sent 'em on to Berlin,
Germany. To read 'em you wouldn't s'pect nothin'—just
mush and all. [*Impressively.*] But they had a way o' doin'
it—a damn sneakin' way. They had a piece o' plain paper
with pieces cut out of it an' when they puts it on top o' the
letter they sees on'y the words what tells them what they
wants to know. An' the Frenchies gets beat in a fight all on
account o' that letter.

COCKY. [*awed.*] Gawd blimey! They ain't 'arf smart
bleeders!

DAVIS. [*seeing his audience is again all with him.*] An'
even if these letters of his do sound all right they may have
what they calls a code. You can't never tell. [*To* DRISCOLL,
who has finished untying the packet.] Read one o' 'em, Drisc.
My eyes is weak.

DRISCOLL. [*takes the first one out of its envelope and bends
down to the lantern with it. He turns up the wick to give
him a better light.*] I'm no hand to be readin' but I'll try ut.
[*Again there is a muffled groan from* SMITTY *as he strains at
his bonds.*]

DAVIS. [*gloatingly.*] Listen to him! He knows. Go ahead,
Drisc.

DRISCOLL. [*his brow furrowed with concentration.*] Ut begins: "Dearest Man——" [*His eyes travel down the page.*]
An' thin there's a lot av blarney tellin' him how much she
misses him now she's gone away to singin' school—an' how
she hopes he'll settle down to rale worrk an' not be skylarkin'
around now that she's away loike he used to before she met
up wid him—and ut ends: "I love you betther than anythin'
in the worrld. You know that, don't you, dear? But b'fore I
can agree to live out my life wid you, you must prove to me
that the black shadow—I won't menshun uts hateful name

but you know what I mean—which might wreck both our lives, does not exist for you. You can do that, can't you, dear? Don't you see you must for my sake?" [*He pauses for a moment—then adds gruffly.*] Ut's signed: "Edith."

[*At the sound of the name* SMITTY, *who has stood tensely with his eyes shut as if he were undergoing torture during the reading, makes a muffled sound like a sob and half turns his face to the wall.*]

JACK. [*sympathetically.*] Hell! What's the use of readin' that stuff even if——

DAVIS. [*interrupting him sharply.*] Wait! Where's that letter from, Drisc?

DRISCOLL. There's no address on the top av ut.

DAVIS. [*meaningly.*] What'd I tell you? Look at the post-mark, Drisc—on the envelope.

DRISCOLL. The name that's written is Sidney Davidson, wan hundred an'——

DAVIS. Never mind that. O' course it's a false name. Look at the postmark.

DRISCOLL. There's a furrin stamp on ut by the looks av ut. The mark's blurred so it's hard to read. [*He spells it out laboriously.*] B-e-r—the nixt is an l, I think—i—an' an n.

DAVIS. [*excitedly.*] Berlin! What did I tell you? I knew them letters was from Germany.

COCKY. [*shaking his fist in* SMITTY's *direction.*] Rotten 'ound! [*The others look at* SMITTY *as if this last fact had utterly condemned him in their eyes.*]

DAVIS. Give me the letter, Drisc. Maybe I kin make somethin' out of it. [DRISCOLL *hands the letter to him.*] You go through the others, Drisc, and sing out if you sees anythin' queer. [*He bends over the first letter as if he were determined to figure out its secret meaning.* JACK, COCKY *and*

SCOTTY *look over his shoulder with eager curiosity.* DRISCOLL *takes out some of the other letters, running his eyes quickly down the pages. He looks curiously over at* SMITTY *from time to time, and sighs frequently with a puzzled frown.*
DAVIS. [*disappointedly.*] I gotter give it up. It's too deep for me, but we'll turn 'em over to the perlice when we docks at Liverpool to look through. This one I got was written a year before the war started, anyway. Find anythin' in yours, Drisc?

DRISCOLL. They're all the same as the first—lovin' blarney, an' how her singin' is doin' and the great things the Dutch teacher says about her voice, an' how glad she is that her Sidney bye is worrkin' harrd an' makin' a man av himself for her sake.

[SMITTY *turns his face completely to the wall.*]

DAVIS. [*disgustedly.*] If we on'y had the code!

DRISCOLL. [*taking up the bottom letter.*] Hullo! Here's wan addressed to this ship—S.S. *Glencairn,* ut says—whin we was in Cape Town sivin months ago—— [*Looking at the postmark.*] Ut's from London.

DAVIS. [*eagerly.*] Read it! [*There is another choking groan from* SMITTY.]

DRISCOLL. [*reads slowly—his voice becomes lower and lower as he goes on.*] Ut begins wid simply the name Sidney Davidson—no dearest or sweetheart to this wan. "Ut is only from your chance meetin' with Harry—whin you were drunk —that I happen to know where to reach you. So you have run away to sea loike the coward you are because you knew I had found out the truth—the truth you have covered over with your mean little lies all the time I was away in Berlin and blindly trusted you. Very well, you have chosen. You have shown that your drunkenness means more to you than any love or faith av mine. I am sorry—for I loved you, Sidney

Davidson—but this is the end. I lave you—the mem'ries; an' if ut is any satisfaction to you I lave you the real-i-zation that you have wrecked my loife as you have wrecked your own. My one remainin' hope is that nivir in God's worrld will I ivir see your face again. Goodbye. Edith." [*As he finishes there is a deep silence, broken only by* SMITTY'S *muffled sobbing. The men cannot look at each other.* DRISCOLL *holds the rubber bag limply in his hand and some small white object falls out of it and drops noiselessly on the floor. Mechanically* DRISCOLL *leans over and picks it up, and looks at it wonderingly.*]

DAVIS. [*in a dull voice.*] What's that?

DRISCOLL. [*slowly.*] A bit av a dried-up flower,—a rose, maybe. [*He drops it into the bag and gathers up the letters and puts them back. He replaces the bag in the box, and locks it and puts it back under* SMITTY'S *mattress. The others follow him with their eyes. He steps softly over to* SMITTY *and cuts the ropes about his arms and ankles with his sheath knife, and unties the handkerchief over the gag.* SMITTY *does not turn around but covers his face with his hands and leans his head against the wall. His shoulders continue to heave spasmodically but he makes no further sound.* DRISCOLL *stalks back to the others—there is a moment of silence, in which each man is in agony with the hopelessness of finding a word he can say—then* DRISCOLL *explodes.*] God stiffen us, are we never goin' to turn in fur a wink av sleep? [*They all start as if awakening from a bad dream and gratefully crawl into their bunks, shoes and all, turning their faces to the wall, and pulling their blankets up over their shoulders.* SCOTTY *tiptoes past* SMITTY *out into the darkness . . .* DRISCOLL *turns down the light and crawls into his bunk as*]

CURTAIN

MATERIA MEDICA

by

FLORENCE RYERSON

and

COLIN CLEMENTS

This sketch dedicated to the nurses of a hospital in Southern California presents a universal problem. Shall the probationer-nurse yield to the strict demands of study or to the impulse of love? The ending is a surprise.

Florence Ryerson and her husband, Colin Clements, lived on a ranch in California. For years this writing couple issued dozens of plays short and long for screen and stage as well as short stories, articles and eight novels.

Their adaptation for the screen of an old children's story, *The Wizard of Oz,* met with wide popular approval. Not so long ago two full-length plays, *Harriet* and *Strange Bedfellows* ran on Broadway for many nights.

Mr. Clements died a few years ago.

COLIN CLEMENTS   FLORENCE RYERSON

MATERIA MEDICA

CHARACTERS

MISS EMMERT

MISS JOHNSON

MARGUERITE, *a probationer*

MISS BROWN

MISS ROSSON

MISS FRANKLIN, *superintendent of nurses*

MISS THOMAS, *her assistant*

SCENE

The corner of a library in a large hospital.

TIME

The present.

The library of a hospital is indicated by a plain white wall with an open window in the middle. A stool stands under the window, with long benches to left and right. Two potted rubber trees, or large vases of conventionalized leaves and flowers, stand at the ends of the benches.

Upon the benches sit four NURSES, *two to the left, two to the right. Their uniforms are white, and stiff with starch, as are the caps which sit perkily upon their heads. In spite of the jauntiness of their caps, they are very, very serious.*

MARGUERITE, *who is little, and young, and blonde, sits upon the stool between the benches. Because she is only a probationer, her uniform is blue and she wears no cap. Her curls, lighted by the window behind her, stand up every which-a-way. Her eyes sparkle, her cheeks are pink, and, entirely contrary to regulations, she wears a red rose, stuck*

111

carelessly in the front of her white apron.

When the curtain rises, each NURSE *is holding an open book, studying Materia Medica. Their concentration has set them into a slow rhythm. They sway slightly from side to side in unison.*

Without lifting her eyes from her book, the NURSE *on the end of the bench at the right puts her book·on her knees and stretches her arms in the air with a bored "Ho-hum." This is repeated by the next* NURSE, *and goes all down the line. They all take up their books again and start studying, this time aloud.*

MISS EMMERT. [*In a sing-song voice.*] "Materia Medica is the study of the substances used in treating the sick. Most of these substances are drugs—"

[*The other* NURSES *take up the chant in turn.*]

MISS JOHNSON. "And the rest are serums, solutions of bacteria, or extracts of organs. The subject may be divided into three distinct branches."

[THE FOUR NURSES *stiffly swing around and stare at* MARGUERITE. *She turns startled eyes from one pair to the other.*]

MARGUERITE. [*In a delightful Southern drawl.*] "They are— They are—" Oh, Lordy me! I don't know what they are! I can't get this stuff to stick in my head! [*With a woebegone expression she runs her hands through her curls.*]

MISS BROWN. [*Severely.*] "They are Materia Medica proper, or pharmacognosy, which deals with the botanical, chemical, or physical properties of drugs."

MISS ROSSON. [*Still more severely.*] "And pharmacology or pharmacodynamics, which is the study of the action or the effects of drugs."

MISS EMMERT. [*Very, very severely.*] "And therapeutics, which deals with the treatment of disease."

MARGUERITE. All right—don't tell me! [*She screws up her face to concentrate better.*] "Drugs are obtained from the mineral, vegetable, and—and— [*Soft music suddenly starts outside the window.*] Oh, that's Dr. West! I know the radio in his car. He's early this afternoon.

THE FOUR NURSES. Sh-h-h! Sh-h-h!

MISS BROWN. [*Stiffly.*] A probationer should be seen and not heard!

MISS ROSSON. And not even seen unless she's sent for.

MARGUERITE. [*Subsiding on her stool.*] I'm s—sorry. [*She goes back into her chant.*] "Drugs are obtained from the mineral, vegetable, and—and—" Oh, dear, what is the third? "Mineral, vegetable, and—"

THE FOUR NURSES. Animal! *Animal!*

MARGUERITE. [*With a sigh of relief.*] That's it! "Mineral, vegetable, and animal kingdoms." [*Beaming.*] See, I knew the answer to that one! [*Her attention is again drawn to the music.*] He's gone—and forgotten to turn off his radio. [*As* THE FOUR NURSES *turn and stare at her.*] I mean Dr. West. I was going to say, I can remember "animal and vegetable kingdoms," but I'm right stupid when it comes to the definition of "solid preparations."

MISS EMMERT. "Powders are crude or other drugs ground up into powder and used in this form."

MISS JOHNSON. "Pills are drugs moulded in the form of a very small sphere."

MISS BROWN. "Capsules are drugs made into a small cylindrical gelatin container."

MISS ROSSON. "Tablets are dried powdered drugs which have been compressed into small discs."

MARGUERITE. There! I think I have it all straight in my mind now. "Materia Medica is the study of—" Don't you love that song? [*She hums with the radio.*] It's simply marvelous to dance to, especially with— [*She stops suddenly, then adds, quaveringly:*] At least—I mean— "Materia Medica is the study of—of—"

MISS EMMERT. "Substances—"

MARGUERITE. "Substances used in—in—"

MISS JOHNSON. "Treating—"

MARGUERITE. That's the word I was trying to think of! "Treating the sick."

[*In spite of herself, her trim little feet are dancing in time to the music, and her body is jouncing up and down on the stool in the same rhythm. All the* NURSES *lean forward to look at her feet. She looks down at them herself, as though seeing them for the first time. They stop dancing and tuck themselves under the stool discreetly.*]

MARGUERITE. "Treating the sick. Most of—of—"

MISS BROWN. "These substances—"

MARGUERITE. "—are drugs and the rest are—are—"

MISS ROSSON. "Serums."

MARGUERITE. Yes. "Serums."

MISS EMMERT. "Solutions."

MARGUERITE. Oh, you needn't have prompted me on *that* one. I know it perfectly! "Solutions." Yes. "Solutions of—of—" [*She looks helpless, then brightens.*] "Solutions of bacteria." Horrid little bugs! "Or—or—"

MISS JOHNSON. "Extracts of—"

MARGUERITE. "Extracts of organs." Organs. [*A far-away look comes into her eyes.*] I just can't help it, but that definition always reminds me of Mendelssohn's—you know. [*She hums a bit of the "Wedding March" against the music outside.*] Um-um-de-dum-dum-dum-dum . . . Here comes the bride—

THE FOUR NURSES. [*One after the other.*] Hush!

MARGUERITE. [*Contritely.*] I'm so sorry! I can't seem to keep my mind on things to-day. I guess it's the music, and the sunshine . . . and the way the trees are blossoming out. I feel like blowing up . . . the way a firecracker does!

[*To express their indignation,* THE FOUR NURSES *close their books with a bang.*]

MISS EMMERT. Well, really!

MISS JOHNSON. I never heard anything—

MISS BROWN. In all my life—

MISS ROSSON. So utterly ridiculous.

[*The* NURSES *all open their books once more and start studying. There is a long pause, while the music plays on.*]

MARGUERITE. [*Looking up from her book again.*] Last night was a beautiful night, too. Did you-all see the moon? [*She giggles.*] I wasn't s'posed to, but I slipped out and looked up at it. Such a baby moon! I looked over my shoulder and made a wish. A very serious wish.

[THE FOUR NURSES *bring their fingers to their mouths.*]

THE FOUR NURSES. Sh-h-h! Sh-h-h!

MARGUERITE. I'll keep quiet—word of honor!

[THE FOUR NURSES *begin murmuring "Materia Medica."* MARGUERITE *goes back to her book and tries to study, but it's no use. She takes the rose from the front of her apron and inhales its fragrance, then speaks dreamily.*]

MARGUERITE. Dr. West looked so handsome in the moonlight—I mean, in the sunlight—I mean, this morning, when he ordered a bar of soap for Number 378. [*She sighs.*] I wonder if he realizes how handsome he really is.

MISS EMMERT. A probationer should never even mention a doctor.

MISS ROSSON. Let alone refer to him as handsome.

MARGUERITE. [*Covering her mouth with her hands.*] Oh, did I say something out loud? I didn't mean to. Truly, I didn't. I was just thinking— [*She looks from one side to the other.*] I was thinking— [*She shrugs her shoulders.*] Oh, well, one *does* think sometimes.

MISS JOHNSON. You should learn to concentrate.

MISS ROSSON. And study your lessons.

MARGUERITE. [*Humbly.*] Yes, Miss Johnson, Miss Rosson.

MISS BROWN. Nursing is not an easy profession.

MISS EMMERT. It certainly is not. An anesthetist, or a surgical nurse—

MARGUERITE. Yes, Miss Brown, Miss Emmert. But I don't want to be an anesthetist. And I don't want to be a surgical nurse. I just want to stay in the maternity ward and take care of babies forever and forever.

MISS BROWN. Please stop talking.

MISS EMMERT. Can't you see you are interrupting?

MARGUERITE. I'm sorry. Really I am. I'll be good. But I can't help thinking of them. Did you see that little pink scrap of a thing on the fourth floor this morning? You did, Miss Emmert. You gave him a bath, and just smothered him with powder. And you hugged him, too. I saw you!

MISS EMMERT. I did nothing of the sort! "A pink scrap of a thing." Indeed!

MISS JOHNSON. A probationer should learn to regard all babies coldly, as patients.

MISS BROWN. And nothing but patients. She should weigh them and bathe them—

MISS ROSSON. And smother, I mean *dust*, dust them with powder.

MISS EMMERT. All in a detached and professional manner.

MARGUERITE. That's exactly the way I do it. [*She picks up her book with a sigh.*] Oh, dear! Powders. Pills. Capsules. Tablets. I'll never, never get them straight. Why don't people just swallow their medicine out of a bottle and save us trouble?

[THE FOUR NURSES *look shocked.*]

MISS BROWN. Really! I don't know what the hospital is coming to!

MISS ROSSON. In my day probationers were meek.

MISS EMMERT. And respectful.

MISS JOHNSON. I'm sure *I* was.

MISS BROWN. So was I.

MISS ROSSON. And I.

MARGUERITE. [*Who has been toying with her rose instead of listening.*] I like red roses best, don't you? They smell so sweet. There was a lovely vase of them in the hall last night. They belonged to Number 378. He's good-looking, too. But not as good-looking as Dr. West—I mean somebody—somebody I met—I mean, I saw in a movie. [*She sniffs the rose again.*] Do you think my nose is funny? Just because it turns *up* at the end instead of down?

MISS EMMERT. I can think of nothing that interests me less than your nose.

MISS JOHNSON. Nothing.

MISS BROWN. Absolutely nothing.

MISS ROSSON. Up *or* down.

MISS EMMERT. And if you don't stop distracting our minds, you will have to leave the library.

MARGUERITE. [*Dreamily.*] That's what *he* said. I distracted his mind. Especially my nose. My eyes and my hair, too, but *especially* my nose.

MISS EMMERT. Well, really!

MISS ROSSON. This is more than human nature can bear!

MARGUERITE. I know, but even doctors can be human—sometimes. I mean, they are just like men. And men are—well, they are, aren't they? Especially when they say good-night.

MISS EMMERT. [*Sharply.*] When who says good-night?

MARGUERITE. Oh, men . . . and doctors . . . and people like that . . . when there's a moon . . . and the radio in 378 is playing . . . and they give you roses.

MISS ROSSON. Are you referring to Number 378?

MARGUERITE. [*Shocked.*] Oh, no! Why, he's married. His wife has twins. At least, he has 'em too, of course. I just mean when . . . oh, when anyone gives you a rose, it's sort of romantic. Even in a hospital.

MISS EMMERT. It is not!

MISS JOHNSON. A hospital is cold and hard.

MISS BROWN. And clean and white.

MISS ROSSON. And extremely aseptic.

MISS EMMERT. But never romantic.

MISS JOHNSON. No, never.

MISS BROWN. Never.

MISS ROSSON. Absolutely *never*.

MISS EMMERT. [*Picking up her book.*] And that is that! We will go back to our work.

[*The other* NURSES *pick up their books and go into their rhythm again.* MARGUERITE *tries to follow their example, but fails miserably.*]

MARGUERITE. [*Dreamily.*] Just the same, it would be wonderful to marry a doctor. He's so noble. I mean, all doctors are noble.

THE FOUR NURSES. Sh-h-h! Sh-h-h!

MARGUERITE. I'm sorry! It's that music, that's what it is. I don't know why everybody always has to make up songs about love. Love. Everything is *love*, and *dove*, and *stars above*. It takes your mind off your work. It makes you think about—

THE FOUR NURSES. Keep quiet!

MARGUERITE. [*Suddenly looking left and right.*] Golly gee! Miss Franklin and Miss Thomas! We sure are in for it!

MISS EMMERT. "Powders . . ."

MISS JOHNSON. "Pills . . ."

MISS BROWN. "Capsules . . ."

MISS ROSSON. "Tablets . . ."

MARGUERITE. [*Takes up her book, closes her eyes, and begins to chant and sway with the others.*] "Powders are— powders are—are crude or other drugs—" [*She looks at her book, discovers it is wrong side up, reverses it, then closes her eyes again.*] "Powders are crude or other drugs —drugs ground up into powders and used in this form. Pills are—pills are drugs—" [*She consults her book.*] "Pills are drugs moulded in the form of a very small sphere."

[MISS FRANKLIN *enters from the right,* MISS THOMAS *from the left. They fold their arms.*]

MISS FRANKLIN. Good-afternoon, young ladies.

[*Four heads with four caps, and one without, nod simultaneously.*]

THE FOUR NURSES. [*One after another.*] Good-afternoon.

MARGUERITE. [*Self-consciously.*] Good-afternoon, Miss Franklin.

MISS THOMAS. Good-afternoon, young ladies.

[*The heads nod again.*]

THE FOUR NURSES. Good-afternoon.

MARGUERITE. [*Absent-mindedly.*] Good-night, sweetheart. Oh! I mean, good-afternoon, Miss Thomas.

MISS FRANKLIN. I trust you have all been making good use of your time.

MISS THOMAS. If you haven't, we shall soon know.

MISS FRANKLIN. Books closed, please.

[THE FOUR NURSES *close their books with a snap.* MARGUERITE *takes one desperate last look, then closes her book, also with a snap.*]

MISS THOMAS. Now, young ladies.

MISS FRANKLIN. Shall we start with capsules, pills, and powders?

MISS THOMAS. Or papers, vescettes, and tablets?

MARGUERITE. [*Impatiently.*] Oh, who cares?

MISS FRANKLIN. Young woman, probationers are here to work and study, study and work!

MISS THOMAS. And they do *not* wear red roses! You will throw it out the window.

MARGUERITE. Oh, no. Please! Let me keep it. I shan't wear it—honestly!

MISS FRANKLIN. Throw it—

MISS THOMAS. Out!

MISS FRANKLIN. At once!

MISS THOMAS. [*Seeing that* MARGUERITE *is hesitating.*] At once.

[*Almost in tears,* MARGUERITE *obeys and tosses the rose out the window. She turns back with a beaming smile.*]

MARGUERITE. It fell on his car! I mean, Dr. West's car.

THE FOUR NURSES. [*One after the other.*] Sh-h-h! Sh-h-h!

MISS FRANKLIN. [*Down her nose.*] Now we shall resume the recitation.

MISS THOMAS. Beginning with powders.

MARGUERITE. Powder!

[*As though reminded of something, she dives into her pocket and brings out a compact. She begins to powder her nose.*]

THE FOUR NURSES. [*Genuinely shocked.*] Oh! [*They stare at* MARGUERITE, *then lower their eyes to their books.*]

MISS FRANKLIN. You will give me that compact.

MISS THOMAS. You will give me that puff.

[MARGUERITE *hands them over.* MISS FRANKLIN *and* MISS THOMAS *step back into their places, their hands behind their backs.*]

MISS FRANKLIN. We shall start with powders.

MISS THOMAS. In unison, please.

THE FOUR NURSES. "Powders are crude or other drugs ground up into powder and used in this form."

MARGUERITE. [*A lap behind.*] "—and used in this form."

THE FOUR NURSES. "Pills are drugs moulded in the form of a very small sphere."

MARGUERITE. "—very small sphere."

THE FOUR NURSES. "Capsules are drugs made into a small cylindrical gelatin container."

MARGUERITE. "—a small something of other continuer."

MISS FRANKLIN. Container.

MISS THOMAS. Container, is the word.

MARGUERITE. Container is the word I *meant.*

MISS FRANKLIN. You seem to have learned to-day's lesson very well.

MISS THOMAS. Very well, indeed.

MISS FRANKLIN. We shall skip tablets, vescettes, and powders.

[*The* NURSES *sigh with relief.*]

MISS THOMAS. Skip tablets, vescettes, and powders.

MISS FRANKLIN. [*To* MARGUERITE.] And begin with you.

MISS THOMAS. The definition of Materia Medica.

MARGUERITE. [*Who has been stretching her neck toward the window and listening to the music.*] Did you say Materia Medica?

MISS FRANKLIN. [*Nodding.*] Materia Medica.

MISS THOMAS. The definition of.

MARGUERITE. Oh, dear me! Now I know it. I'm sure I do! Yes. "Materia Medica deals with the botanical, chemical, and physical properties of love." Oh, that can't be right, can it? "Properties of—of—drugs." You see? I did know!

MISS FRANKLIN. [*Unconsciously she begins to hum the song the radio is playing, then catches herself and stops suddenly.*] And pharmacology?

MISS THOMAS. [*She, too, catches herself swaying to the music and stops suddenly.*] Or pharmacodynamics.

MARGUERITE. "Is the study of the actions or the affections" —I mean—"the affects of—of drugs."

MISS FRANKLIN. And therapeutics?

MARGUERITE. [*Quaveringly.*] Therapeutics?

MISS THOMAS. Therapeutics.

MARGUERITE. "Deals with the treatment of husbands"—no, that isn't it—"with the treatment of disease and—and—" [*Wailing.*] I don't know what's the matter with me! I'm all mixed up in my mind!

MISS FRANKLIN. [*Nodding left and right.*] Young ladies, you are dismissed.

THE FOUR NURSES. [*Rise, and speak, one after the other.*] Thank you, Miss Franklin.

MISS THOMAS. And return to your wards.

THE FOUR NURSES. [*One after the other.*] Thank you, Miss Thomas.

MISS FRANKLIN. [*As* MARGUERITE *rises.*] *You* will remain.

MISS THOMAS. And study.

MARGUERITE. [*As the other* NURSES *go out, two right, two left.*] Yes, Miss Franklin. Yes, Miss Thomas. [*She sits down again.*]

MISS FRANKLIN. Try to fix in your mind that a nurse's life is dedicated to duty.

MISS THOMAS. And nothing *but* duty.

MARGUERITE. Yes, Miss Franklin. Yes, Miss Thomas.

MISS FRANKLIN. Any frivolous thoughts—

MISS THOMAS. Should be sternly repressed.

MARGUERITE. Yes, Miss Franklin. Yes, Miss Thomas. [*She looks offstage, right, and brightens.*] Oh, there's Dr. West. He's leaving!

MISS FRANKLIN. [*Reaching into her pocket and bringing out the compact.*] Did you say Dr. West?

MISS THOMAS. [*Bringing out the puff.*] Dr. West?

[*They straighten their hair, their caps, their aprons, and hurry out, one left, the other right.*]

MARGUERITE. [*Trying desperately to keep her mind on her work.*] "Materia Medica . . . study of the substances . . . powders are crude or other drugs . . . pills . . . small spheres . . . cylindrical gelatin container . . ." [*She can't help glancing over her shoulder toward the window.*] "Tablets are pow- dered . . ." [*Someone calls "Who-hoo," very softly.* MAR- GUERITE *stops, then goes back to her book.*] "Tablets are powders . . . or powders are pills . . . or I don't know whats . . . compressed into something or other . . . and tablets are—" [*The "Who-hoo" comes again. She rises, and stands at one side of the window, then calls, in a very low voice to someone outside.*] Yes. Yes, Doctor, this is me. Yes, I'm all alone. I took that bar of soap to 378, like you told me to. What? Oh, Doctor, but I can't go. You know very well it's against the rules, especially with a doctor. They wouldn't ever let me come back. What? You don't want me to come back? What? *What?* [*Her eyes open very wide.*] Marry you? When? Oh, that makes all the difference in the world! [*She whirls around twice, throws her book into the air, tears off her apron, wads it into a ball, tosses it on the floor and does a crazy dance around it, then she scrambles over the stool and up on to the window sill.*] Yes, Doctor! Yes! Yes!

[*She disappears through the window. The music swells for a moment.*]

CURTAIN

THE UGLIEST MAN IN THE WORLD
by

ARCH OBOLER

One of the most popular radio writers is Arch Oboler. His words have the explosive force of bullets.

Born in 1909, Oboler grew up in Chicago where he aimed to become a naturalist. For years he collected all sorts of scientific specimens. Later he enrolled at the University of Chicago in a course of electrical engineering. Nonetheless he always wished to write.

In 1938 Oboler brought with him to New York from the Chicago studio of NBC the script here offered. In it Oboler employed the style known as interior monologue or the stream-of-consciousness. He is the author of over 600 original and powerful radio dramas, flesh-creeping at first like "Lights Out," but later turning more realistic. So successful has he been that he has been imitated by other radio writers. In addition, since 1941, five of his plays have won national awards after having been acted by such distinguished players as Bette Davis, Nazimova, James Cagney, Ronald Colman, Raymond Massey, and Olivia de Havilland.

His "Fourteen Radio Plays" is the first of a series to contain radio plays by one author.

Reprinted by special arrangement with the author. Text from *"Oboler Omnibus."*

ARCH OBOLER

RADIO'S MASTER SCREEN-WRITER.

THE UGLIEST MAN IN THE WORLD

ANNOUNCER. Scene—a room in semi-darkness. At a table sits a man—tall, gaunt, his heavy face lit occasionally by a random beam of light reflecting off the polished barrel of a revolver. This is Paul Martin; as the revolver twists in his nervous fingers, the thoughts in his mind twist and turn . . . twist and turn. . . .

PAUL. [*in a "stream-of-consciousness" semi-monotone.*] . . . gun in my hand gun in my hand in all my life I never had a gun in my hand smooth gun hard gun cold gun in my hand bullet won't be cold warm bullet hot bullet burning hot hot as the blood—no, can't think of that lift the muzzle of the gun up hole as black as where I'm going turn the muzzle up and press the trigger trigger cold against my finger cold as death but life is colder—rhythm to that—poet dies with final rhythm poet dies who never wrote a poem—headline for the tabloids—Poet Dies with Final Rhythm.

VOICE. [*in distant background; it has a thin, rasping quality.*] Ugliest Man in the World a Suicide!

PAUL. [*firmly—spacing words as if to drive the previous thought out.*] Poet-Dies-with-Final-Rhythm!

VOICE. [*in close.*] Ugliest Man in the World a Suicide!

PAUL. [*louder, in anguish.*] Poet Dies in Final Rhythm!

VOICE. [*in close—shouting.*] Ugliest Man in the World a Suicide! [*Repeats again simultaneously with:*]

PAUL. [*in time with above shouting as if to drown it out.*] Poet Dies in Final Rhythm!

VOICE. Ugliest Man in the World a Suicide!

PAUL. No, no, stop! Stop!

[*Voice stops knife-clean.*]

PAUL. [*down—in agony.*] Ugliest Man in the World! All right, I'll think the thing for the last time tear the words around in my head over and over the way they've torn for thirty years! Ugliest Man in the World. Ugliest Man in the World. Ugliest Man in the World! Press the trigger and stop it press the trigger! No, no, I can't! Got to wait! Wait for what? For nothing! Nothing if I press the trigger nothing if I wait! Press the trigger . . . NO! [*Pause.*] My chance . . . yes my chance to think . . . think it all out clearly for the first time in my life . . . how it started why it's ending *this* way . . . think it all out clearly from the very start . . . *then* press the trigger—

MOTHER. School today, Paul.

PAUL. There's a start—first day of school—how old was I— nine or ten—she kept me home away from others—I didn't know why until that day she said:

MOTHER. [*with a note of regret in her voice.*] School to- day, Paul.

PAUL. I said:

BOY. [*Paul as a boy of about ten, a bright-voiced lad.*] All right, Mother!

PAUL. She took me to school—into a room full of more children than I'd ever seen—I was so happy I wondered why her face was white and set—she said:

MOTHER. [*nervously.*] Miss Edwards, this—this is my son. . . . I—I want him in your class. Please—be kind to him.

PAUL. Before the teacher could answer Mother hurried out of the room and left me there. The teacher's eyes were on me—small eyes, worried eyes, thin mouth opened—turned to the faces lifting below her—

TEACHER. [*fading in fast with slight echo.*] Your attention, children! I—I want you to meet a new classmate. His name is—uh—

BOY. Paul Martin!

PAUL. For a moment not a sound—row on row of children looking up at me, staring up at me, gaping up at me. . . . And then—

[*Sound of a single child's laughter beginning in distant background, painting the picture of one of the school children in the room involuntarily bursting into laughter at the sight of the new classmate's face.*]

PAUL. One of them started laughing!

[*Sound of another child's laugh joining the first—one by one other children join in until the room rings with derisive shrill laughter of children.*]

PAUL. [*through the laughter, dazedly.*] Another laughing —another—and another! Laughing, laughing, I stood there a little boy looking down at their twisting mouths my ears filled with the sound of them! Making fun of me I knew that, but *why? Why?*

[*Laughter stops knife-clean.*]

CHILD'S VOICE. [*whispering derisively.*] Ugliest boy in the world!

PAUL. [*down.*] Ugliest boy in the world . . . that's why you kept me away from children, Mother, kept me away until you didn't dare to any longer. [*Agonizedly.*] Oh, Mother, Mother, before you let others see me why didn't you close your hands around my neck, put a knife in my heart, drown me, bury me, put me away where eyes couldn't see me—

[*Sound of small boy crying heartbrokenly, continuing behind.*]

PAUL. But you didn't, so this was my boyhood—tears, tears without end—a boyhood of tears, a boyhood of tears. . . .

[*Sound of crying of small boy's voice fading out, then:*]

PAUL. Took me out of school—kept me away from all the

others—what good was it? I knew, I *knew!*

VOICE. [*whispering.*] There wasn't a mirror in the house!

PAUL. Not a mirror—I didn't dare you didn't dare—until that day you died!

MINISTER. [*fading in fast.*] We have committed your beloved to the keeping of the mother earth which bears us all. Cherish the memory of her words and deeds and character. [*Fading.*] Good night, my boy. . . .

PAUL. Alone . . . so quiet in the house . . . I sat down. . . . So quiet. . . .

[*Sound of ticking of clock, continuing behind.*]

PAUL. And then suddenly as if the clock were talking to me—yes, I remember—[*in time to tick-tock of clock*]. Look—at—your—self, look—at-your—self! Look—at— Yes!

[*Sound of tick-tock stops knife-clean.*]

PAUL. Look at myself! That's what I'd do! Never had looked at myself—never had seen what I looked like—I hadn't dared, I hadn't wanted to but now I had to know—had to, had to! A mirror—had to find a mirror—surely Mother had kept one mirror somewhere!

[*Sound of opening of drawers and shuffling through miscellaneous objects.*]

PAUL. Drawer after drawer—a mirror, surely there was a mirror. Mother gone, I was alone, a life to make, my face perhaps it wasn't—

[*Sound of drawers stops with*]

PAUL. A mirror—yes—there was one wrapped and hidden where she thought I'd never find it! Tore the paper off!

[*Sound of tearing paper.*]

PAUL. I kept my eyes shut until the glass was clear—and then I *looked!* [*Cries out in mingled horror and anguish.*] Ahh!

[*Sound of crash of glass, painting picture of his flinging the mirror to the floor.*]

PAUL. [*low.*] My face . . . can I bear the memory of my face? Can I think of it even now gun in hand? Yes, I will, I will! What did I see—what is my face—[*His voice now becomes strained and tight with repressed anguish.*] A brow? No brow! A thing that sloped away sharply—quickly—like a peaked roof half fallen in! Nose? A thick wad of ugly flesh protruding out between two close-set eyes! My eyes— my eyes—Mother of God, my eyes! Two tiny red-rimmed green-flecked globes that stood far out beyond the lids and twinkled like a fat round pig's! My eyes! *That* was why they laughed at me! My eyes!

VOICE. [*derisively in close.*] Ugliest Man in the World!

PAUL. Yes . . . I was that. . . . No longer boy—ugliest *man* in the world. . . . Not even tears could help me now. . . .

[*Sounds of busy street continuing in distant background.*]

PAUL. The world outside—at last I had to go out into it— make a living—get a job.

[*Street sounds rise, then continue behind.*]

VOICE. Job? You want a job?

PAUL. Job. . . .

VOICE. Work for *me?* Hah!

PAUL. [*more hopelessly.*] Job. . . .

VOICE. Say, ya think I'm runnin' a circus side-show?

PAUL. Job.

VOICES. [*in alternation with increasing tempo.*] Get out! . . . Circus side-show! . . . Get out! . . . Circus side-show! . . . Get out! . . . Circus side-show! Side-show! Side-show! [*In close.*] Side-show!

[*Sound of circus—calliope, crowds, etc., painting a picture of a circus lot. We hear the spiel of a barker far back. All this fades in background and continues behind.*]

BARKER. [*in background.*] Step up, ladies and gents, step up! The one and only—*etc., ad lib.*

PAUL. [*in a way that belies his words.*] Wasn't bad there . . . no . . .

BARKER. [*fading in fast.*] . . . that's what I said, come on ladies and gents, that's what I said the Ugliest Man in the World! At only a dime! The very small part of a dollar! [*Fading.*] Something to talk about, something to tell your children and your grandchildren when you get home—you saw the Ugliest Man in the World! That's it, step closer, closer, closer. . . . [*His voice fades and continues behind.*]

PAUL. [*slowly.*] Didn't mind . . . after a while. . . . Faces looking up at me again—staring, whispering, getting their dime's worth—spieler talking—faces staring—whispers—snickers—didn't mind, why should I? I could get away from them! Yes, stand there in the noise and laughter—and leave them far behind! Leave the smell of them and the noise of them and the twisting faces of them. Shut my eyes and leave them! Quickly! Quickly!

[*All the sound of the circus and the barker's spiel fades out as we hear music fading in, music painting a picture of green sun-drenched fields with clouds drifting lazily overhead.*]

PAUL. [*slowly, reminiscent happiness in his voice.*] I'd be in a field, sun-drenched—face to the sky, the warm sun touching me, soft grass cushioning me, my arm outstretched—all around me such peace and loveliness. . . . I'd lie there so happy . . . and then a breeze touching my face . . . and a small white cloud in the sky . . . then another—[*wonder in his voice*] and all at once the clouds were like a woman's face looking down at me! . . . A woman. . . .

[*Music stops knife-clean.*]

PAUL. [*all his loneliness in his voice.*] A woman!

[*Circus sounds, continuing behind.*]

WOMAN. [*hard, cheap.*] Hullo, big fella!

PAUL. [*startled.*] Uh—uh—hello . . .

WOMAN. Helluva day, uh?

PAUL. Y-yes . . .

WOMAN. Sure give you a big play—I mean the yokels—don't they?

PAUL. Y-yes . . .

WOMAN. Me, I'm with Sammy Morton—you know, the grind show.

PAUL. I—I—

WOMAN. Not one of the strippers, y'understand! I do a high-class dance—you know—a semi-classical! . . . Sure been a long, hot day, ain't it?

PAUL. It—it has . . .

WOMAN. Nice walking out—in the dark . . . I mean the—the air's kinda different than on the Midway . . . Yeah, nice in the dark. [*In close.*] Awful nice. . . .

[*Sound of circus background rises slightly, then stops with*]

PAUL. [*not quite as vibrantly as before.*] There was a woman . . .

[*Sounds of wind sighing, continuing behind.*]

WOMAN. [*with a throaty intimate quality in her voice now.*] Let's stop walkin'. . . .

PAUL. [*low.*] All right. . . .

WOMAN. [*sighing.*] Ah, it's nice, ain't it?

PAUL. [*hesitantly.*] Do—you like the moon?

WOMAN. Moon? Sure, sure! You been workin' in tent-shows long, big fella?

PAUL. So complete, the moon. . . .

WOMAN. Boy, you sure pack 'em in! I heard tell you sell more pictures than anybody in the show! Dimes sure add up, don't they?

PAUL. I—I don't think of money very much. . . .

WOMAN. [*hastily.*] Oh, me, I don't either! I just like people or I don't—who cares what they got?

PAUL. It's—it's very kind of you . . .

WOMAN. Kind? What d'ya mean?

PAUL. You . . . me. . . .

WOMAN. Yeah?

PAUL. [*slowly.*] Your face . . . did you ever look down from the clouds?

WOMAN. [*laughs throatily.*] Ya mean have I ever been high? I'm high now. . . . [*Intimately.*] I like the dark, big fella.

[*Countryside sounds rise as transition, then fade out slowly.*]

PAUL. [*saying the words flatly now.*] There was a woman . . .

[*Circus sounds fade in and continue behind.*]

PAUL. Talking . . . they were talking . . .

WOMAN. [*laughing throatily.*] Yeah, yeah, sure, Sam, what d'ya take me for—a chump? . . . [*Her voice hardening.*] Well, what do you think? His face makes me sick just to look at him . . . but he's got a pocketful of dough! [*Chuckling.*] My face in the clouds—that's good, eh, Sam? So I keep lookin' up, and I don't have to see *his* mug! So we get along fine and last week, so last week I got a telegram from my mamma—[*chuckling.*] poor mamma and the mortgage—and yesterday while he was looking at me up in the clouds I got another handful o' bucks and maybe in a couple of weeks I—[*She breaks off sharply with*]

[*Sound of closing door—all background of circus noises stop.*]

WOMAN. [*gaspingly.*] You! . . . [*There is mingled fright and bravado in her voice.*] All right, so ya heard! So what? . . . What're ya starin' at? I don't like your face! You heard me—I don't like your face!

PAUL. [*tensely.*] I gave you—

WOMAN. You gave me a couple o' laughs! That's all a face like yours is good for—for the laughs!

PAUL. Love. . . .

WOMAN. Love! [*Laughing uproariously.*] D'ya hear that? Love? D'ya think any woman could love a mug like yours? It's not a face—it's a mug, a puss, a pan! Yeah, ya hang it up in the dark and scare kids with it for Hallowe'en! Go on, beat it, get outta here! No more walks with me, big fella! I've a bellyful o' laughs and I— [*In sudden fright.*] Hey, what're ya—no, stay away from me! Don't—ah—[*Her voice breaks off with: sound of loud slap of open hand against face.*]

[*Sound of train, behind.*]

PAUL. Go on—beat it—get out! Yeah—get out as far as I could get out!

[*Train sounds, low after a few seconds and continuing behind.*]

PAUL. Any place—

[*Train sounds rise, then continue behind.*]

PAUL. Anywhere—

[*Sound of click-clack of railroad ties behind.*]

PAUL. Any place, any place—anywhere—anywhere—get away, get away—get away, get away—

WOMAN. [*through rail-tie effect.*] It isn't a face—it's a mug, a pan, a puss! [*Laughing viciously, fades.*]

[*Sound of train effects rises for a few seconds, then stops.*]

PAUL. Get away! [*In low semi-monotone.*] Yeah, got away—good and far away—fields—grain—a farm—they didn't care what kind of face—just work hard . . . work—work—work, hour after hour, sweat salt on my lips, work, keep working, you don't think when you work, hour after hour, day after day! The sun over the fields frying your brain—[*exultantly*] and I couldn't think, I couldn't think it was good I couldn't think! But I'm thinking now—gun in my hand—stop that thinking—gun in my hand—*no!* Got to think out my life—think it out clearly. . . . Think of that day . . . *she* waved at me. . . .

[*Music begins; warm, sun-drenched behind.*]

PAUL. Was working . . . bent over . . . sun hot on my back . . . grain thick around me filling the world, covering, hiding me. . . . I straightened up. Something moving through the grain on the road, climbing the hill so far away could hardly tell just what it was. Shaded my eyes from the sun. [*Tensely.*] I saw! A woman on horseback! No, so small—must be a girl. I saw her arm wave at me! I dropped in the grain! I hid! Leave me alone! Leave me alone! Leave me alone!

[*The music rises for a few seconds, then continues behind.*]

PAUL. The next day again! Standing in the grain—a tiny figure on horseback—waved at me! I dropped in the grain again! No! No more! Just the sky and the grain and the work was all I wanted!

[*The music rises for a few seconds, then continues behind.*]

PAUL. The next day and the next—a girl on horseback riding far off there on the road—waving at *me* in the grain! Waving at me day after day—and one day I—I didn't drop in the grain. I stood—I waved back at her.

[*The music rises slightly, then stops sharply.*]

PAUL. Waving at me . . . because she couldn't see me . . . see my—

WOMAN'S VOICE. [*back—fading in and out fast.*] Face—puss—pan—mug! . . .

PAUL. So she waved at me . . . and I waved back . . . and soon I was waiting for that moment in the day when she'd pass in the distance and her arm would lift toward me. . . . I waited for that . . . just waited. . . . Then I was thinking about her all the time—I had so much time to think in my loneliness! What did she look like—*what did she look like?* I—I don't remember how—in spite of myself one day I was hiding in the grain at the edge of the road—waiting—for her. . . .

[*Sound of horse's hoofs approaching, fading in behind.*]

PAUL. [*tensely.*] Wanted to run yet I stayed! . . . Wanted to cover my eyes yet I looked! . . . Looked with eyes as big as all my loneliness!

[*Sound of horse ambling slowly along; the horse suddenly snorts.*]

PAUL. Horse knew I was there . . . she didn't . . . She started singing a little song as she passed—a song without meaning—warm as the sun. . . .

GIRL. [*sings a wordless, happy little song, fading out with the sound of the horse's hoofs.*]

PAUL. And I saw! [*With wonder in his voice.*] I saw her! Face as lovely as mine was ugly! Young—lovely—young—lovely—the words tumbled over and over in my head as I watched her go by! Young and lovely! . . . I began to see *her* face everywhere in the grain, in the sky and at night in the dark.

VOICE. [*whispering.*] *Ugliest Man in the World—*

PAUL. . . . Thinking of the loveliest face in the world. I tried to stop but I couldn't! The loneliness in me was a pain I couldn't endure any more!

[*Sound of horse's hoofs fade in and out together with the girl singing her wordless little song.*]

PAUL. Again and again I hid in the grain and watched her go by me. Just a quick moment—and then she was gone—and I was left in loneliness again. . . . But I couldn't meet her—I knew that one look at my face and she'd scream—she'd run—yes even laugh! Laugh, laugh, and if she laughed I knew my world would end—crack in the laughter and crush me under! . . . [*Low—broodingly.*] If she couldn't see my face. . . . Yes, if she were blind! Read a book like that somewhere—woman never saw the man she loved—if *she* couldn't see *me!* Only know me as I am, my voice, my thoughts, my dreams, ambitions! *If she couldn't see!* Dangerous dreams—day-dreams—that brought me to a gun in my hand . . . [*With misery in his voice.*] But I had nothing! So I had dreams of her, blind, not knowing my face! Not knowing and her face close to mine and her lips. . . . I said it, yes I said it over and over again—Mother in Heaven—if she were only blind! *If she were only blind!* [*With self-horror in his voice.*] Wish father to the deed—that day working in the grain—looked up—she was riding by—so early—why so early? Her little hand waving at me—then the rush of an auto—

[*Sound of shriek of auto brakes, far back, together with the scream of the girl.*]

PAUL. [*breathing heavily.*] I ran, the grain tearing at me —holding me back! In a moment she was in my arms!

GIRL. [*shock and confusion in her voice.*] Help me—please help me! I can't see! [*On a rising tearful note.*] I *can't see!*

PAUL. [*after a pause—slowly, down.*] Can't see! I dreamed it, prayed and now—

GIRL. [*tearfully in background.*] I can't see!

PAUL. [*in close.*] What have I done? What have I done?

VOICE. [*fading in and out fast.*] Concussion—nerve block—

PAUL. [*confusedly.*] No, I—I had nothing to do with it—just a thought—I—I had only *thought!* But now she couldn't see me . . . as I was! [*In growing exultation.*] *Couldn't see me!*

GIRL. [*fading in fast.*] You've been very kind to me, Mr. Martin—Paul—

[*Music begins, singing behind.*]

PAUL. Music—everlasting music in my ears!

[*The music rises, then continues behind.*]

GIRL. Come here every day, won't you?

[*The music rises, then continues behind.*]

GIRL. It's so good having you to talk to. . . .

[*Music rises, then continues behind.*]

GIRL. You've made these wonderful days, Paul!

[*Music rises joyously and continues behind.*]

PAUL. Music—everlasting music—her voice—being with her—knowing her—and she—

[*Music rises, then continues behind.*]

GIRL. You've such a good mind, Paul—the best I've ever known, I needed a mind like yours!

[*Music rises, and laughs joyously behind.*]

GIRL. [*laughing happily.*] I'm laughing, Paul, because you've made me happy again—you, Paul—and I—I bless you for it!

[*Music rises in a fast quicksilver movement behind.*]

PAUL. Happy days—endless days—quicksilver days—then *the* day. . . .

[*The music stops suddenly, ominously.*]

GIRL. [*fading in fast.*] Paul, I've been waiting for you!

PAUL. [*the love of her in his voice.*] I wanted to be here sooner but the grain . . .

GIRL. [*laughingly.*] The grain! Is it very tall and bold now, Paul?

PAUL. Very!

GIRL. Remember how the grain used to keep us apart? Before I even knew you! I'd wave and the grain was between us, and I never knew you!

PAUL. [*in close.*] Is knowing me . . . important?

GIRL. [*lovingly.*] Paul . . .

PAUL. Do you know me now?

GIRL. You're the only one I've wanted to be with me. . . .

PAUL. *Do* you know me now?

GIRL. You know so little about me to ask me that. . . .

PAUL. You're . . . lovely. . . .

GIRL. My family . . . why I came to live out here alone. . . .

PAUL. So very lovely. . . .

GIRL. Paul—Paul, listen to me! I know you now better than I could if my eyes were open and twice as wise as they ever could have been!

PAUL. You're lovely. . . .

GIRL. And so are you. . . .

PAUL. [*slowly.*] You've never seen me. . . .

GIRL. When people have talked together as much as you and I . . . every little hope and hurt, dream and plan . . . don't they know more than if they looked at faces? And what *do* you look like, Paul?

PAUL. I—

GIRL. No, let me guess! I've sat here in the dark and seen your face so many times before me!

PAUL. My face . . .

GIRL. Yes, let me tell you! It's a large virile face—a face that matches up with all the strength of you! Strong straight mouth, firm chin, skin brown yet soft, straight nose that's not too small—[*laughing softly*] yet not too large! And then your eyes—

PAUL. Eyes!

GIRL. Oh, yes, your eyes! I'll tell you about your eyes! They're large and dark . . . and gentle . . . gentle as the way of you, Paul. . . . Well, how close was I to knowing you?

PAUL. [*with effort.*] Give me . . . your hand. . . .

GIRL. No, no! I don't want to touch your face!

PAUL. You—

GIRL. Later, yes, but not now, Paul! I want you to read me something!

PAUL. Read—

GIRL. Yes, so strange we were talking about faces when I've had this book for you to read me. One of my favorites —of a man with courage! Look—do you know the book, Paul?

PAUL. [*begins to read.*] "Cyrano de—" [*Breaks off.*]

GIRL. Yes, brave Cyrano de Bergerac! You've read the play, of course?

PAUL. I—I never have. . . .

GIRL. Then I envy you! I wish I'd never read it so that I could read—hear it all over again! Please read it for me— start any place! . . . Read it, Paul!

PAUL. [*begins to read slowly.*] "Thou lovest her? Tell her!

For I do surmise thou art a hero in her eyes!"

GIRL. That was Le Bret! Cyrano's friend! Now go on, read Cyrano's speech!

PAUL. [*begins to read again with slowly increasing difficulty.*] "Nay. Shall I woo the loveliest maid in France—look at me, friend, with my poor big devil of a nose—I dream, even I, of walking 'neath that beam, loving, beloved. As I dream my soul expands, exults, but soars to fall. I see my profile shadowed on the wall."

GIRL. You read it with your heart, Paul. . . .

PAUL. He was . . . ugly?

GIRL. The rest of him was beauty—just his nose. . . . Read Cyrano's lines and I'll try to remember Roxane's. She was the woman he loved, and he never dared tell her of his love because of his ugliness. Read, Paul—the top of the page! Roxane calls "Sister! Oh, Sister!" Read, Paul!

PAUL. [*reading.*] "No, call no one here. Ere you come back, I should have gone away. I longed for harmony to end my day."

GIRL. [*in close.*] "I love you! Live!"

PAUL. "In fairy tales, long since, the princess said that, and the ugly prince lost all his plainness in that sudden sun. But, see! I finish as I was begun!"

GIRL. "I made your grief, I, I!"

PAUL. "You made my bliss. I lacked all woman's kindness . . . even this. . . . My mother found me ugly. And I had no sister. Lest they mock an ugly lad, I shunned all women. You became my friend. One soft gown brushed my path before the end."

GIRL. And then the moon comes out and Le Bret says, "Thy other love!" Cyrano loved the moon!

PAUL. "Welcome, fair friend above."

GIRL. "I loved but once, and twice I lose my love!"

PAUL. [*brokenly.*] "I loved but once, and twice I lose my love! . . ."

GIRL. Paul! You . . . cry? . . .

PAUL. Cry? What is there to cry about?

GIRL. It's true! There's no reason to cry! Just a play—in life no man could be such a fool!

PAUL. [*softly.*] Goodbye. . . .

GIRL. Goodbye? No, no, don't leave me, Paul! I haven't had a chance to tell you! Tomorrow *I* go!

PAUL. [*slowly.*] You?

GIRL. My family . . . I'm strong enough to be moved now. . . .

PAUL. Where—

GIRL. Paul, we've talked so much of anything and everything but never of this! My eyes—an operation—I'll see again! That's why I didn't want to see your face with hands! I'll see you with my *eyes,* Paul! [*Fading.*] See you with my eyes! See you with my eyes!

PAUL. [*building.*] See again! See again! See *what?*

[*Sound of children laughing in background.*]

PAUL. A face to laugh at!

VOICE. Ugliest Man in the World!

PAUL. A face to jeer at!

WOMAN. [*in background.*] A puss—a pan—a mug!

PAUL. Face to shout at! [*Brokenly.*] But not to love! Not to love! "Never will I, so long as I am master, let beauty so divine meet such disaster—ugliness mar perfection." Cyrano, I read you a thousand times because *she* read you! The author gave *you* a paper nose, but my ugliness is flesh and blood! Flesh and blood! Flesh and blood to see, to hate—

she'll never see me never never! Lift the muzzle, press the trigger trigger cold against my finger cold as death but life is colder thoughts in my mind like a whirling circle!

VOICES. [*whispering over and over.*] Ugliest Man in the World—Ugliest Man in the World—

PAUL. [*through the above.*] Press the trigger, press the trigger, press the trigger— [*Gasps with:*]

[*Sound of door opening in background.*]

GIRL. [*back.*] Paul?

PAUL. [*low and tensely.*] Who is it?

GIRL. [*fading in fast.*] Paul!

PAUL. Ah! . . .

GIRL. Paul, where's the light?

PAUL. You see!

GIRL. It's been weeks—I've been searching—where's the light, Paul?

PAUL. Forget me!

GIRL. So dark—in your hand—what—[*As she feels gun.*] Oh, Paul!

PAUL. I wasted too much time thinking . . .

GIRL. [*tears in her voice.*] Oh, my dearest!

PAUL. Forget me, I tell you! You knew me in the dark—. well, now it's light for you, and I'm not meant for light! Forget me!

GIRL. I want to know you . . . in the light . . . your ugliness. . . .

PAUL. [*sharp intake of breath.*]

GIRL. Yes, Paul, I've known—first when you cried with Cyrano . . . then I asked the others, and they told me. . . .

PAUL. But you don't know! My face! A thing—

GIRL. A thing apart, as my blindness was apart from me. I love you . . .

PAUL. You . . . love. . . .

GIRL. Love you! Yes, yes! I love you!

PAUL. You . . . don't . . . know. . . .

GIRL. But I *will* know! Turn on the light, Paul. . . . [*Vibrantly.*] Turn on the light! I love you! Live! For *me!*

PAUL. [*slowly, in wonder.*] "In fairy tales, long since, the princess said that and the ugly prince . . . lost all his plainness in [*glowingly*] that sudden sun!"

Musical Curtain

QUARE MEDICINE

by

PAUL GREEN

This amusing one-acter of Carolina folk comes from the pen of one of our best regional playmakers. Paul Green studied with the famous Prof. Koch of the University of North Carolina, where he wrote his early plays for the Carolina Playmakers. Out of his intimacy and knowledge of the common folk, black and white, from his own region, he has written honestly and poetically of the share-croppers, tenant farmers, and prisoners. His Pulitzer Prize play, *In Abraham's Bosom*, written in 1926, pictured the struggles of a Negro son of a white man who dreams of improving the condition of his race. Equally notable are *Hymn to the Rising Sun*, *The House of Connelly*, *Johnny Johnson* and a series of symphonic dramas which employ the aid of music. Paul Green teaches philosophy at the University of North Carolina in Chapel Hill.

PAUL GREEN

QUARE MEDICINE

CHARACTERS

OLD MAN JERNIGAN.

HENRY JERNIGAN, *his son.*

MATTIE JERNIGAN, *Henry's wife.*

DOCTOR IMMANUEL, *a patent-medicine vendor.*

TIME—*Several years ago at the close of a winter day.*

PLACE—*A farmhouse in eastern North Carolina.*

THE *scene is the combined sitting-room and bedroom of the* JERNIGAN *house, with a fireplace to the left, a sewing-machine to the right and a table in the center of the room. The floor is carpeted with bright straw matting, and everything bristles with tidy primness. A door is at the center back and one at the left rear. The window at the right center, neatly curtained, shows a streak of sombre autumn fields filling up with the blue dusk of a fading winter day. From another part of the house the voice of a woman can be heard shrilly singing "Rescue the perishing, care for the dying." The elder* JERNIGAN, *walking with a stick, comes carefully in at the rear door shivering with cold and carrying a mug-cup in his hand. Below a mass of white hair his face shines out like a ruddy autumn apple, and his whole person suggests the toughness and durability of a dried hickory root.*

Half-way across the room he stops and listens to the singing.

JERNIGAN. [*Sharply imitating.*] "Rescue the perishing, care for the dying!" [*He moves over to the fire and sets his mug to warm; after which he takes a bottle from the mantel, pours out some medicine in a spoon and swallows it. He sits down and stretches his hands to the blaze with a grunt of satisfac-*

149

tion. In a moment he feels the cup and takes a long drink. The woman's voice calls from off the right.]

VOICE. Father!

JERNIGAN. [*Starting.*] Ah-hanh! What is it?

VOICE. [*Nearer.*] Father—fath—er!

JERNIGAN. [*Moving towards the door at the left.*] What is it, Mattie?

VOICE. Supper's 'bout ready. Where's Henry? [*The singing begins again, fading towards the kitchen.*]

JERNIGAN. [*Calling futilely after her.*] He's feeding up and'll be here in a minnit. [*He listens awhile and then reseats himself thoughtfully before the fire. Presently there is a heavy scraping of feet on the steps outside and* HENRY JERNIGAN *comes timidly in at the rear. He is a big awkward farmer of thirty or more, hesitating and shy. He takes his seat silently and wearily in a rocking chair, being careful not to touch the whitewashed hearth with his feet. The old man looks at him closely.*]

JERNIGAN. Tired out, ain't you? Hyuh, try some o' this 'simmon beer, I jest dreaned the barrel.

HENRY. [*In a slow, fumbling voice.*] I don't want none o' that, I believe.

JERNIGAN. Unh-hunh. [*They both lapse into silence, staring before them. Soon the elder* JERNIGAN *peers through the window at the winter sunset.*] Gonna be cold, Henry, cold. Robins been flying towards the south all day. [HENRY *says nothing.*] You're tireder'n common, ain't you, Henry?

HENRY. Yeh. [*Lifelessly.*] Wore out, wore out.

JERNIGAN. [*Taking his bottle from the mantel.*] Hyuh, take this last dost of Doctor 'Manuel's tonic. [HENRY *shakes his head.*] Well, I will then. [*He pours out the last drop and swallows it.*] Doctor said he'd be by today. 'Bout night and he ain't hyuh yit. You better git him to give you something, ye better, Henry, you're looking thin, thin.

HENRY. He ain't no doctor, he's a humbug.

JERNIGAN. Lard help my life!

HENRY. Wonder that mess don't kill you—old branch water and chemicals he's mixed up, I betcha. [*He sighs heavily, listening to the song in the kitchen.*] That old man's crazy with his poetry and talking and medicine!

JERNIGAN. Hunh, not hardly. [*Solemnly.*] 'Tain't body tired what ails ye, Henry, is it? [*After a moment he jerks his thumb in the direction of the song.*] Still singing, Henry. There it is.

HENRY. Yeh, I know.

JERNIGAN. Ah-hah, but folks will marry jest the same. She's worse'n ever, Henry. Good she is, religious good. Cooking and sewing and scrubbing and all fixed up fer tonight. Look over there on the machine at what she's got finished fer them there Hindoos or whatever they are. There's my coat I bought in Dunn five years back at Old Man Ransome Taylor's sale!

HENRY. [*His eyes travelling heavily about the room.*] What's she got on fer tonight?

JERNIGAN. Another one o' them there meetings. Old Mis' Pate and her gang's coming hyuh to sew fer the heathen and them that's starving over in the old world. [*Staring at him intently.*] This religious mess is gonna kill Mattie off ef you don't git up manhood enough to stop it. Sing and talk, sing and talk, Lard, I caint stand it no more.

HENRY. I—I caint—I ain't gonna put my authority on nobody. She's her own boss.

JERNIGAN. Own boss! She's her own boss and our'n too. Well, ef you're scared of her, all right. They ain't no help fer it. [*He turns towards the fire, patting his foot forlornly on the floor.*] But, Henry, ye ain't gitting no fun out'n living, and right now's the time ye ort.—And as fer me—I been wanting to talk—[*Hitching up his chair.*]—to you 'bout this. Why the name o' Old Scratch you don't up and putt down yer foot I cain't see. [HENRY *says nothing.*] But ye won't. [*Half to himself.*] He ain't got no backbone, lets everybody run over him. [*He reaches for his cup and drains down the last of his beer in an angry gulp.*] Ye didn't git that from yer mammy ner from me, Henry. [*He mocks the singing in the kitchen.*] "Rescue the perishing—"

HENRY. [*Suddenly standing up.*] I cain't have no row with nobody, not with her nohow, I tell you. [*At the door.*] I got to go part the cow and calf. [*He slams the door behind him and the old man jumps in astonishment.*]

JERNIGAN. Dinged ef he didn't slam the door—hee, hee, hee. Good fer you, Henry, good fer you! [MATTIE, *a fair faced young woman, comes in from the left, singing and carrying a stone churn in her arms. Despite her housewifely certainty of action, there is an indefinite feminine frailty about her.*]

MATTIE. What's good for Henry?

JERNIGAN. [*Hurrying in confusion to his chair.*] Nothing, Mattie, nothing at all. [*She looks sharply at him a moment and then sets the churn by the hearth.*]

MATTIE. I'm putting the milk here to turn. I wisht you'd look at it every now and then and stir it with the dasher.

JERNIGAN. All right, Mattie, all right.

MATTIE. And mind, don't you spill none o' that old beer on the hearth.

JERNIGAN. I won't, Mattie, I won't.

MATTIE. What'd Henry go out for?

JERNIGAN. To git the calf away from the cow.

MATTIE. [*The words piling out.*] I bet he didn't wipe his feet when he come in. And did you? [*Staring on the floor and following* HENRY's *trail.*] No, he didn't—just look at the dirt, just look at it. [*She hurries into the room at the left and returns with a broomsedge broom.*] Here, sweep it up, Father. [*She pushes the broom into his hand.*] I've got to go back to my batter. [*She sticks her head out the door at the rear and calls.*] Henry—Hen—ry! Supper! [*She turns back into the room and old* JERNIGAN *falls to sweeping.*] Sweep it towards the hearth, towards the hearth, Father, and mind the milk, don't git it full of dust. [*She goes out singing, beginning where she left off.*]—"from sin and the grave—"

JERNIGAN. [*Sweeping.*] Lard, Lard A'mighty, was ever martel man so persecuted! [*Leaning on his broom and musing.*] There he is— [*Nodding his head to the right.*]—pore soul, not at peace in his own household, going about like a man with the mulligrubs, cain't sleep, cain't eat, worried, worried down to the ground. And there she is—[*Nodding to the left.*]—reading the *Christian Herald* and hearing about dirt and disease and famine over in Azhy till she ain't fit to live with. Listen to her, listen to her, will you? What's to become of me, Old Moster only knows. What, to come to this, to this in my old age and me—[*Thumping on his chest.*] —yeh, me, old and with a crippled leg from marching in Furginny! [*He wipes his sleeve across his eyes and goes back to sweeping. Presently he stops and begins to muse again.*] Putts me to sweeping, she does, and churning and gitting up the eggs, and following old setting hens around. And she's had me at the wash-tub like an old woman, she has. Damn it! [*His voice sags over the oath.*] I ain't no woman. If Henry ain't got the grit to say something, I have. It's "Father do this, Father do that, Father—Father—Father!"

But ding it all, she's a good girl. It's that drot'n old bell-cow of a Bella Pate and her gang what's got her worse'n she ever has been. I wisht a starm would come up and blow the whole shooting-match of 'em clean to Roosia or wherever it is. Then they'd git enough o' them there heathen, I reckon. But they ain't got no right to interfere with me, not a bit. [*He puts a hand into his pocket and holds up a small tin box in his left hand and a plug of tobacco in his right.*] Here they come and set 'pon me about my tobacco. Chew chewing-gum, chewing-gum, they say, to save for the heathen and to per-tect my health. [*He rattles the tin box.*] And I've chewed that wad o' stuff till I cain't git rid of it in my sleep. Cain't wear it out, cain't by no means. I'm done of it, I am. Have to slip off and hide to chew my tobacco, and all in a land o' freedom. [*He stands thinking, then goes to the door at the left and calls.*] Mattie, air ye busy?

MATTIE. Yes, I've got my hands in the dough!

JERNIGAN. All right. [*He stealthily bites off a chew from his plug, drops his tin box back in his pocket and spits in the fire with grim happiness. Just as he is leaning to spit a second time, the door opens suddenly at the left rear, and* MATTIE *comes in with a cloth. Old* JERNIGAN *draws back, and begins sweeping in a flurry of embarrassment. He calls out testily.*] Thought you was busy. Ain't I doing all right?

MATTIE. Sweep it clean, Father. I forgot this cloth for the churn. [*She raises the lid from the churn and stirs the con-tents around with the dasher.*] It's all right and ready, lack-ing just a bit, for churning. Don't you let it slosh on anything while you're a-churning it. [*She wraps the cloth around the handle of the dasher. The old man is sweeping and watching her out of the corner of his eye. While she is bent over she sees something on the hearth that attracts her attention. She rises up to her height and with a sharp note in her voice turns upon him.*] Mr. Jernigan— .

JERNIGAN. Nah, nah, Mattie.

MATTIE. Signs don't lie, and there's signs of it there on my hearth. [*Working around the room and watching him furtively.*] Right here in my front room! Ain't you got your mouth full of tobacco right this minute? [*He shakes his head.*] Yes, you have, yes, you have. [*She stands looking at him as he sweeps.*] Father, why don't you say something, cain't you talk? [*He makes little movements of agony and finally chokes.*] Yes, yes, you are chewing right now. Spit it out, spit it out! Don't stand there and swallow that juice, it'll kill you. [*In desperation he runs to the fireplace and explodes into the fire, and stands coughing with a nauseated look on his face.*] I'll get you some water! [*She hurries out and reappers immediately with a glass of water and a battered wash-basin full of claying material.*] Here drink it, and take this pan and rag and clay the hearth over. [*After drinking the water, he ruefully gets down on his knees and begins work. She goes to the machine.*] Hurry and get it done, I got supper nearly cooked. [*She sits down and begins sewing and singing* "How firm a foundation—"]

JERNIGAN. [*Indicating the garments.*] Air they fer the heathen?

MATTIE. They are that.

JERNIGAN. [*Timidly.*] 'Course you know best, I reckon. But how you know they wear britches over there?

MATTIE. [*Staring at him in amazement.*] Who ever heard of folks not wearing britches! You know they'd put 'em in jail for such, if they didn't.

JERNIGAN. [*Venturing.*] I hearn they don't wear nothing over there but a string around their waist to tell where the middle is.

MATTIE. [*Pedalling furiously.*] You men don't care, of

course, care 'bout nothing but your farming and your crops. Why, it's in the *Christian Herald* where the little children just go through the woods in big droves gnawing the bark of the trees they're so hungry. We've decided to give up our breakfast and send the cost of it to them.

JERNIGAN. That's why you didn't eat breakfast this morning. Well—you et a whole lot more for dinner to make up fer it, didn't ye?

MATTIE. [*Sharply and with a nervous note in her voice as she gets suddenly up from the machine.*] Father, take all this mess out when you get done—that old 'simmon beer cup, and that old 'Manuel patent medicine bottle, and don't forget to carry the clay pan out—[*She goes out at the left. Her song is heard rising in the distance. Old* JERNIGAN *continues claying the hearth, muttering to himself.* HENRY *comes in at the rear.*]

HENRY. [*Stretching his legs out carefully towards the fire.*] What's the matter with the hearth *now*?

JERNIGAN. [*Setting the pan in the corner by the wood-box.*] Nothing, nothing, Henry. She thought she saw a speck on it somewhere.

HENRY. You must a-been chewing tobacco ag'in.

JERNIGAN. Well, why shouldn't I chew it?

HENRY. Yeh, yeh, I wisht you could in peace.

JERNIGAN. You'd be better off ef you'd go back to chewing.

HENRY. I know. But I promised her I'd quit and I have.

JERNIGAN. I used to chew it 'fore it quit raining in Africky or wherever it is and 'fore old Bella Pate brung her sanctified self around here, I did, and they was some joy in having a far then, and some reason for having a farplace too. [*Tapping on the andiron with his stick.*] That's what it's made fer—to spet in.

HENRY. [*Timidly and somewhat hopefully.*] Why don't you talk it out with Mattie. [*Earnestly.*] I wisht you would.

JERNIGAN. Durned ef I didn't come purty nigh telling her something a while ago. [*He catches* HENRY *by the arm.*] Now look-a here, Henry, you'n me's got to do something. The thing for you to do is to walk down the road tonight and meet Mis' Pate and them folks and tell 'em they cain't come up here to carry on no prayer-meeting and sewing business. Tell 'em to go som'r's else. Tell 'em to go to—hell!

HENRY. [*Shrinking away.*] I cain't do that, I cain't. Lord, you're near 'bout gone to cussing.

JERNIGAN. And tell 'em yer wife ain't gonna have nothing else to do with sich.

HENRY. [*Quickly.*] I tell you what, you do it.

JERNIGAN. I would in a minnit, Henry, but you're the head o' the house and you better, it's yer place to. [HENRY *turns himself about before the fire.*]

HENRY. Mebbe they won't come tonight, and before they meet another time mebbe we can figger on something to do.

JERNIGAN. Hunh, they'll be hyuh, all right.

HENRY. [*Staring off.*] I hear they's mad dogs about. One bit at Dick Ryall's child this evening.

JERNIGAN. [*Studying.*] Well, that may break up the meeting, but I won't believe it till I see it, not me. Take more'n mad dogs to stop religion. You stand up to Mattie, I tell you, putt the britches on and wear 'em yourself. Lard, I cain't understand you. Why you let her impose on me in my old age the way you do I cain't see. [*He turns away and sits down in his arm-chair.* MATTIE *comes in with a tin bucket in her hand.*]

MATTIE. I've got to go across the fields to Mis' Ragland's a bit— [*Suddenly stopping.*] Henry, go right back out that door and wipe off your feet.

HENRY. [*Mumbling.*] I thought I cleaned my feet. [*He goes outside and is heard scraping his shoes on the edge of the porch.*]

MATTIE. Sweep it up, Father. [*He gets the broom and sweeps.*] I got to borrow some soda from Mis' Ragland and she wanted me to bring her a jar o' jam.

HENRY. [*Coming back into the room.*] I'll go over there for you, Mattie.

MATTIE. No, I'll go, and you-all go on and git your supper. I've put the biscuits in the stove, and they'll be ready by the time you wash and get to the table. Now, Henry, don't let them biscuits burn. [*She goes out.*]

JERNIGAN. [*Scornfully.*] Jest look at her—didn't have a bit o' business over there, jest wants to go over see what old Nonie Ragland's got made up for the heathen. Henry, you got to lay the law down, I tell you.

HENRY. Yeh, yeh.

JERNIGAN. Now, I'm gonna talk straight to you. Women is like mules and all dumb brutes, Henry, you got to break 'em 'fore they'll work.

HENRY. Nah, nah, I cain't do that. [*There is a knock on the porch.*]

JERNIGAN. Who kin that be? [*Happily.*] That's my doctor, I betcha. [*The knock is repeated at the door.*]

HENRY. [*Raising his voice in sudden irritability.*] Go on away! Go 'way!

JERNIGAN. [*Staring at him.*] What— Come in, come in! [DOCTOR IMMANUEL *comes in.*] I knowed it was you, Doctor, I knowed it was you. [*The* DOCTOR *is a man of medium height, about fifty years old, dressed in a cheap threadbare dark suit, celluloid collar and dark tie. His coat hangs low*

*and nearly to the knees, clerical-like. Despite his cheap dress
there is an indefinable air of distinction about him; something
scholarly, something forlorn in his pale clean-cut face and
dark piercing eyes. He carries a well-worn medicine case in
his hand. As he enters the door, he pulls off his derby hat,
disclosing a huge mop of long black hair streaked with gray
and resting like a bolster on his neck and shoulders.]*

DOCTOR. *[In a deep level voice.]* Masters of this house,
friends—

JERNIGAN. *[Pushing up a chair.]* Come right in, come right
in and make yourself at home. *[The* DOCTOR *lays his hat on
the bed at the right and puts his case in a chair. He moves
in a sort of dream-like, mask-like manner, intent upon his
business and paying little attention to the two men.]*

DOCTOR. *[His voice moving in a level chant, half-singing
as he opens his case.]* What can I do for you tonight? What
can I do for you tonight? *[He takes out bottle after bottle,
shakes it, squints at it towards the light, and replaces it,
chanting as he does so.]*

> As you all know, wherever I go,
> My name is Immanuel,
> I treat you well, I make you well,
> Sound as the sweet church bell.

[He turns suddenly on old JERNIGAN *who starts back in
surprise.]* Now what is it, brother? What can I do for you?

JERNIGAN. *[Fetching his bottle.]* Another bottle. I just
drunk the last.

HENRY. *[Growling.]* Another bottle of stump water, dish-
water, rainwater.

DOCTOR. *[Holding up the bottle.]* Doctor Immanuel's Universal Remedy! Right it is and very fit. Distilled from secret
weeds and herbs by mystic processes. Cures internal ail-

ments, cuts, burns, bruises, is an antidote for poisons, can be taken internally or externally. For swelling in the joints, leg sores, sore throat, convulsions, dizziness, fits, and general disorders. [*The words roll from him in a flood. He turns towards old* JERNIGAN, *fixes him with his eyes, and suddenly sings out.*] What is your trouble, brother? Are you healed, better or— It's cold tonight, cold tonight, and ice on the pools in the lane.

JERNIGAN. In my knee, you remember, in my knee. [*He slaps his hand to it.*] I'm getting better, doctor, slowly, slowly.

DOCTOR. [*Holding his hand up in assurance.*] Slowly but surely, certainly, absolutely. Another bottle and you walk straight as any man.

> As you all know, wherever I go,
> My name is Immanuel.
> I always make you well,
> As any man will tell. . . .

[*His voice drops to a whisper and he hums under his breath, the while he is putting away the empty bottle and getting out another. He hands the bottle to old* JERNIGAN.] The price is one and a quarter now, brother. Prices have gone up, prices are going up. The demand exceeds the supply. [*Again he chants.*]

> I travel from morning till night
> Curing and fixing things right.
> From night until day
> I'm on a-my way—

[*He begins placing his bottles back in his case.*]

> Seeking the saddened sight—

[*Again he whirls upon the old man.*] Is the knee all that

troubles you? Have you other troubles, diseases of the body
or the soul?

JERNIGAN. [*Shaking his head quickly.*] Nanh, nanh, I'm
all right saving my knee.

DOCTOR. [*Picking up a small bottle and holding it lovingly
before him.*] Now here is a remedy, *the* remedy, the heart
and soul of the matter, the help for the world's evils. Down
in Egypt, the country of darkness, it was discovered. Dug
out of the tombs of the powers of evil. Hid away they had
it, but my agent discovered it, sent it to me, here it is. [*Reading.*] Dr. Immanuel's Egyptian Tonic. [*Suddenly barking
like an auctioneer, as* HENRY *jumps in his chair.*]

> Two dollars a bottle, two dollars,
> Going at two dollars.
> Are you weak and heavy laden,
> Sore distressed, sad distressed?
> It will cleanse of evil passion,
> Restore you bowels of compassion,
> Accidents, diseases chronic—

[*Shouting.*]

> The marvelous Egyptian Tonic.

[*He sticks it out at old* JERNIGAN.]

> Two dollars once, two dollars twice—
> Going at two—

JERNIGAN. [*Backing away from him as he fumbles in his
pocketbook for his money.*] Nanh, nanh, this bottle's enough.
Here's yer dollar and a quarter. [*The* DOCTOR *takes the money
impersonally.*] Come up to the fire and warm yourself.

HENRY. [*Looking at old man* JERNIGAN *significantly.*]
Anh-hanh, what'd I tell you? [*The* DOCTOR *closes his case and
goes to the bed for his hat.* HENRY *calls to him bitterly.*]

You better look out down in that creek for mad dogs.

DOCTOR. [*Turning back quickly with dignity.*] Mad dogs?

HENRY. Yeh, dogs that are mad. Mad dogs. One of 'em bite you and you'll be madder'n you are now.

JERNIGAN. Yeh, you git bit and you'll foam at the mouth and gnaw bedposts and cut up terrible like Sarah Williams done 'fore she died. She run out in the yard and screamed, and they tried to ketch her but she run off and lay down by the hedgerow and died biting her legs and arms and barking like a dog.

DOCTOR. [*Quickly taking a tiny package from his case.*] Doctor Immanuel's Mad Stone, good for all bites and poisons. Bring it near the afflicted spot and it seizes upon it—[*Clapping it to the top of his hand.*]—and sucks out the poison. Five dollars apiece, five dollars. [*Gazing at it fondly.*] This mysterious stone was taken from the belly of a bewitched deer, killed by the old prophet of the Cape Fear. [*Barking again.*] Five dollars apiece, five dollars, going at five dollars.

[*He pushes the stone quickly out at old* JERNIGAN.]

JERNIGAN. Nanh, nanh, I ain't run mad.

DOCTOR. Five dollars— Five dollars once, five dollars twice —five dollars— [*Suddenly he stops and stares at* HENRY *as if perceiving something remarkable and strange about him. He mechanically wraps up the stone and drops it back in the case, never taking his eyes from the young man. He moves toward him and walks obliquely around him. Old* JERNIGAN *watches him with open mouth. As the doctor approaches him,* HENRY *turns and follows him suspiciously with his eyes.*]

HENRY. Hyuh, hyuh, what you up to? [*The* DOCTOR *continues to stalk him. He draws back dramatically and points a sharp finger at* HENRY.]

DOCTOR. [*Grotesquely.*] Trouble.

JERNIGAN. [*Jumping and giggling nervously.*] Trouble, hee-hee!

HENRY. [*Staring at him.*] Trouble?

DOCTOR. [*His words beginning to pour out in a roll.*] I see upon that brow suffering. My name is Immanuel. I am needed, needed here and now. [*Looking at him in anguish.*] You are weak and heavy laden. Tell me. Speak forth your heart. I am come that ye might have rest from your suffering. Speak forth, thou unbeliever.

HENRY. Hyuh, hyuh, I ain't gonna have no monkey shines. [*With a touch of entreaty in his voice.*] Stop it now.

DOCTOR. [*Shaking his head mournfully.*] I must help you. I feel the call of pain. Speak forth your heart.

HENRY. [*Turning towards old* JERNIGAN.] What's he up to nohow?

JERNIGAN. Now, now, you needn't ax me. [*There is a long silence while the* DOCTOR *stares fixedly at* HENRY.]

HENRY. [*Looking anxiously about the room and presently bursting out.*] I tell you to stop looking at me thataway!

DOCTOR. Trouble, trouble, suffering in the countenance of that face! [*Imploringly.*] Speak, speak, I have remedy for suffering. I can help and aid thee. [*He clasps his hands and waits.* HENRY *stirs uneasily in his chair and old* JERNIGAN *teeters nervously on his feet, beating his thighs with the back of his hands. At last old* JERNIGAN *explodes.*]

JERNIGAN. Well, you air in trouble, Henry!—In a way ye're in the deepest sort of trouble. [*Muttering.*] Me too, and me too.

DOCTOR. [*Triumphantly.*] Ah—hah! Speak, speak!

HENRY. [*Half in wrath and half in perplexed fear.*] Well,

what'n the name of Old Scratch[1] you want?

DOCTOR. Speak forth the evil that is possessing thee.

HENRY. [*Twisting about.*] You tell him, Pa, if they's any evil to be told.

JERNIGAN. Him and me's been seeing a right smart o'worry lately. We was talking about it before you come.

DOCTOR. I know, I perceive it.

JERNIGAN. [*Going on haltingly.*] As the scripture puts it, he's married to a wife. [*He stops.*]

DOCTOR. One had his land, one had his yoke of oxen, another had his wife and could not come. As set forth in the gospel according to Luke.

JERNIGAN. [*Eagerly.*] That's it, doctor, his wife's tuk possession of everything hyuh.

HENRY. Now, now.

JERNIGAN. Well, she has. And that there doctor kin help you, I done told you he could. [*He steps nimbly out into the room and sweeps it with his arms.*] Look a' there, will you? Look at that there h'a'th. Clean as a sheet. And the floor and everything. A speck o' dirt got no home hyuh and we ain't nuther. [*Pointing to the sewing-machine.*] And look over there at that there sewing. My good coat and britches gone fer good, all fer the heathen over the water.

HENRY. You mought stop trying to tell everything.

JERNIGAN. Well, you tell it then.

HENRY. Go on then and say what you wush.

JERNIGAN. All right and I will as shore as you're born. That's just it, doctor, she's plumb tuk with religion and sweeping and talking.

DOCTOR. Where is the lady of the house?

[1] The Devil.

JERNIGAN. Off, off.

DOCTOR. A common case, a common case. The man must stand up and be the master. The scripture tells as much.

JERNIGAN. [*Jubilantly.*] There you air, Henry, there you air. [*Jerking his thumb at* HENRY.] But he won't, he won't, not him. He sets lak a wedge in the rain and takes it every bit. Big as a house he is and ain't got no backbone in him more'n a sack.

DOCTOR. Timid? Afraid? Lacking in manly courage?

HENRY. [*Wrathfully.*] Go on and have it your way!

DOCTOR. Doctor Immanuel will provide. He can cure.

JERNIGAN. You cure 'em both and I'll pay you. Fix it so's I kin chew my tobacco in peace and here's a five dollar bill fer ye. [*He pulls out his pocketbook.*]

DOCTOR. I shall cure them, I must cure them, I *will* cure them. Amen!

JERNIGAN. Do that and this here's your'n. [*He flaps a bill in his hands. The* DOCTOR *begins to pace up and down the room, pushing back his hair and mumbling to himself.*]

DOCTOR. [*Snapping.*] When will the lady of this house return?

HENRY. She just stepped acrost the field. But you needn't be planning none of your mess, I ain't gonna take no part in it.

DOCTOR. Mess! Mess! [*He resumes his walk.*]

JERNIGAN. [*Becoming excited.*] I dunno what you gonna do, Doctor, but I jest beccha you do it. [*Gleefully.*] I bet he does, Henry. Yeh, she'll be right back.

DOCTOR. No sooner said than done. [*Whirling upon* HENRY.] I can cure you both. I can bring peace and order into this distracted home. I can make a man of might out of you. I can make you a mighty man in Israel, both in deed and in

word. I can bring back humility and love to the erring
woman's heart. Yea, [*Lifting up his voice.*] I can prepare a
proper helpmeet for you in your distress. [*Thundering and
glaring.*] But—but—have you faith in my powers?

HENRY. I dunno— I dunno— Hah, crazy!

JERNIGAN. [*Ecstatically.*] Try to raise up yer faith, Henry.
[*Grinding his hands in excitement.*] Hurry up, Henry, hurry
up, she's gonna be back in a minute.

HENRY. [*Shaking his head weakly.*] I'm scared of all this
business. How I know he won't kill me or something or hurt
her.

DOCTOR. Kill! Hurt! [*His jaw falling open in amazement.*]
Alas, young man, your words are wild, wild and full of poison
to my kindly heart. [*His tone suddenly changes to anger.*]
Take your own benighted way then. I offer you peace, you
choose strife. So be it. [JERNIGAN *grasps* HENRY's *arm in
supplication.*]

JERNIGAN. Henry, Henry, try it, try it, boy!

DOCTOR. [*Raising a warning hand.*] But listen, before I
depart over the creek.—[*To himself.*] A mule there swelled
with the colic— Behold salvation is at hand and you refuse it.

JERNIGAN. Air ye crazy, Henry? There he is now going off.

HENRY. [*Beginning to show an unwilling interest under the*
DOCTOR's *spell.*] Well,—

DOCTOR. [*Picking up his hat.*] I shall say no more.

JERNIGAN. Henry, Henry, don't let him go off like that
there! [*The* DOCTOR *picks up his case and moves towards the
door.*]

HENRY. Well, if you're shore you won't hurt me ner her, I
mought—

DOCTOR. [*Apparently no longer interested in him.*] Well,
goodnight and may you endure your punishment as befits

a sufferer so blind. [*He grasps the door knob.*]

JERNIGAN. Henry, Henry!

HENRY. Are you shore you won't hurt me?

DOCTOR. Faith! Have you faith?

HENRY. [*Standing up with sudden decision.*] Well, I'll try it then, by God! Where's your medicine? Bring it on. [*With an amazingly agile bound the doctor springs back into the room.*]

DOCTOR. Saved! Saved! [*He opens his case and searches in its depths. Extracting two tiny bottles, he holds them up in his hands.* HENRY *sits down again watching him with open mouth.*] Ah, here they are, Doctor Immanuel's Cure for the Unhappy Soul. The one is red, the other gray. The red is for the rich blood of manhood. Drink it and you become masterful, fearless, a tamer of the weaker sex. They will bow down to you, worship you, feed upon your words of wisdom as upon honey-dew. Let the woman drink the gray and the man the red. He becomes the lord of his house and his goods. She becomes the meek and lowly helpmeet. There she sits by the fire silent, gentle and sweet. There he sits her master, her lord.

JERNIGAN. [*His eyes shining.*] Listen at him, Henry, listen at him talk.

DOCTOR. [*Lifting up the red vial.*] I remember, I remember. I see in the past. It is a night of storm. The moon is sick and pale and wasting in the west.

> The pale moon doth rain,
> The red moon doth blow,
> It bringeth water in its beak.
> The white moon doth neither rain nor snow.

I rise up in my dreams. Doctor Immanuel comes forth from his couch at the midnight hour, for now it is the time to seek

for the cure of unhappy souls. Silently I go through the
forest towards the appointed place. The rain and the wind
they comfort me on my journey. I go forth alone in the forest,
under the watchful heavens. The signs are right in the sky,
it is the time of the bull, and the bull means life and more
abundant life. [*He waves his hands before his face and
treads up and down the room acting out his journey.* HENRY
and old JERNIGAN *stare at him as if mesmerized.*] I go by
the elder bush in the pathless swamp, I touch the sorrel tree,
and place my hand upon the bark of the smooth bay tree. I
mount the hill and taste of the sweet sassafras and a bit of
the bitter pine, and I, Doctor Immanuel, as the cocks begin
to crow, come to the place of the silent old man and he waits
for me. He has had his dream. Together we go far to the
east, he with six dried sticks of the bloody mulberry and I
with six of the nameless bush under our arms. We come
where the young strong man died for love and his rich red
blood ran into the ground. There we set the pot and build
the fire. [*His voice takes on a hypnotic monotone and he
moves back and forth in the room with the queer unreal steps
of a jumping-jack.*] And into the pot Doctor Immanuel casts
his one and two and three. And likewise the silent one casts
his one and two and three which shall not be named till time
is done. The bottles are brought forth and filled. The silent
old one to his home again which none but two can find. And
Doctor Immanuel forth into the world to heal the distressed.
[*His voice dies away and he hums to himself.*]

HENRY. [*Breaking from the spell.*] Ain't he crazy right?

DOCTOR. [*Picking up the gray vial and throwing up his
hand.*] And hark! [*He stands with his hand uplifted, and
they wait.*] It is night, a night of peace. The farmer sleeps
his toil away, and the stock rest in the stall. The seeds wait
in the earth, in the warm ground. The poor birds sit in the

hedgerow and the snake goes not forth to prey. And now the old moon sleeps in the new moon's arms, hanging in the heavens above the three dark pines. [*Again he falls to striding up and down the floor.*] Doctor Immanuel is forth from his couch. The signs are right. The virgin walks in the sky. He comes to the three dark pines and waits in prayer. And the three maids of the deep swamp minister unto him, they minister unto him. Out of the darkness they come with song and with dancing, their heads hanging low and their rings shining and their garments flashing silver with the flames of gold. [*He turns and stares at* HENRY *who watches him groggily.*] From the mud of the turtle and the scaly snake they come, rising out of the deep night time, out of the mire and swampy slime, where the owl and the bat and the fever are. They rise, bringing the cure, the gray cure, the draught of humility, of peace. [*He stares at the gray vial and stands lost in thought. Presently he turns, his voice humming.*] Drink the red and be filled with life and power; drink the gray, become the meek and gentle of the earth. Doctor Immanuel has said his say! [*He begins walking back and forth across the room.* HENRY *and old* JERNIGAN *stare at him as if fascinated. Far off a woman's voice is heard singing. It draws nearer, and* MATTIE *passes around the house, singing "Rescue the Perishing," and goes into the kitchen.*]

HENRY. [*Swallowing hard.*] Hyuh, they's something quare!

JERNIGAN. He's gonna cure you, Henry. He is! Sink yer trust in him, Henry!

DOCTOR. Come, drink the drink! [*He closes his case and sets the two bottles on top of it.*] Call the lady of the house. She shall have the gray.

HENRY. [*Starting from his dream, sidling up to the bottles, and staring at them suspiciously.*] Mought be something in it, mought not. [*A queer unreal smile breaks over his face*

and he comes up to the doctor and stares at him intently.]
All right, dinged if I don't do it. Dinged if I don't! [MATTIE'S
sharp insistent voice is heard in the kitchen.]

MATTIE. Father! Fathe-er-r! Henry! Henr-y!

JERNIGAN. Drink it, swallow it down, Henry! Can't be no
worse'n [*He turns and mocks* MATTIE.] Father! Henry! and
[*singing.*] "Rescue the pershing—" Go on, Henry.

[HENRY *picks up the red vial, uncorks it and smells it and
sets it down, then takes up the gray one and does likewise.*]

HENRY. Why it don't smell like nothing a-tall.

DOCTOR. [*Stopping in his walk and looking at him pierc-
ingly.*] Bid the lady of the house come in.

HENRY. [*Throwing his head about and beating himself as
if trying to fight off the* DOCTOR's *influence.*] You call her, Pa.
[*The door flies open at the left and* MATTIE *springs in with
a pan of burnt biscuits in her hands.*]

MATTIE. [*In a shrill nervous voice.*] Look what you've
done, both of you. I told you not to let the biscuits burn.

[JERNIGAN *looks at* HENRY *and* HENRY *looks at him.*]

JERNIGAN. [*Finally.*] I thought Henry was looking after
them biscuits.

HENRY. [*Fumbling.*] I didn't even think of 'em, Mattie.

MATTIE. I know, I know. That's just the way it is. That's
just the way it is. That's always the way it is.

DOCTOR. Madam, lady of this house!

MATTIE. [*Starting back.*] Oh, I didn't see you, Doctor
'Manuel. Put some wood on the fire, Father. When'd you
come, Doctor 'Manuel?

DOCTOR. Madam, when you appeared in the door we were
in the midst of a most momentous question.

MATTIE. What'n the world is all this to-do about? You'll

have to tell it quick, I've got to hurry and get supper. We are sewing here tonight—[*With a weary, defiant look towards* HENRY *and old* JERNIGAN.]—sewing for the heathen.

DOCTOR. Madam, after tonight you will not bother about the heathen. You have enough trouble in your own household. We are solving that momentous question.

MATTIE. What in the world is all this to-do about, I ask you?

DOCTOR. [*With high dignity.*] Madam, behold the two bottles there. The one is red, the other gray. The red is for your husband, the gray for you.

MATTIE. Needn't think I'll drink any of your crazy mess.

DOCTOR. The husband will drink the red and take charge of his household. You will drink the gray and obey him in what he says hereafter.

MATTIE. The Lord help my life! [*Turning to* HENRY.] Have you gone out'n your head same as him, to be taking on to such stuff?

HENRY. [*Timidly.*] Try and drink a little bit, Mattie. It won't hurt you! He says it's good for you.

MATTIE. The dog's foot!

HENRY. [*With a hint of determination in his voice.*] He's done said if I drink that stuff you won't know me for another man. [*Decisively.*] And I've said I'll drink it.

DOCTOR. He's going to drink his and you're going to drink yours.

MATTIE. That I'm not. I've never heard of such. Henry Jernigan, you must be crazy to fool with him.

HENRY. Yes, I'm gonna do it. I'm plumb tired of sich a mess of things. I'm gonna change it or die a-trying. [*With a lunge he grabs one of the bottles and throws the contents down his throat.*]

MATTIE. [*Screaming.*] Henry, it'll poison you! [*Henry stands tasting with his lips. A foolish smile breaks over his face.*]

HENRY. Why, it ain't no more'n—

[*The* DOCTOR *brings his hand down on* HENRY's *shoulder with a whack and stares significantly at him.* HENRY's *eyes gradually narrow in comprehension and he turns and walks back and forth across the room thinking. The* DOCTOR *moves around as if unconcerned. Suddenly* HENRY *springs into the air with a yell. Old* JERNIGAN *starts back and falls over a chair.*]

JERNIGAN. Lard, Lard a-mercy!

MATTIE. [*Running up to* HENRY.] Henry, Henry, honey, what is it?

HENRY. [*Tearing wildly around the room and shrieking.*] I'm pizened, pizened! Help, water, I'm afar inside. [*He doubles over in pain.* MATTIE *pursues him wringing her hands. All the while the* DOCTOR *walks ecstatically and yet unconcerned around the room, carrying on his automaton-like actions and his monologue.*]

DOCTOR. [*Chanting.*]

> As you all know, wherever I go,
> My name is Immanuel.
> I treat you well, I make you well,
> As sound as the sweet church bell.
> Down the road I travel,
> Going in rain or shine,
> Healing the sick and afflicted,
> No medicine like unto mine.
> This I tell who comes like Immanuel.

HENRY. [*Falling into a chair and slobbering heavily at the mouth as he gasps.*] Pizened! Pizened! Help, water! [MATTIE *throws her arms around his neck.*]

MATTIE. Run, Father, run and bring the bucket of water. [*The old man shoots into the kitchen and back like a streak. All the while* MATTIE *is crooning over* HENRY *and rubbing his face and forehead feverishly.*] Oh, darling, honey. What can I do? [*She breaks into wild sobs.*]

JERNIGAN. Hyuh, hyuh, drink some water, Henry. [HENRY *springs out of his chair, knocking* MATTIE *from him. He souses his head in the bucket and drinks, spits out great mouthfuls of water on the floor and empties the bucket over his head. Then he stamps the bucket to pieces, shrieking and yelling.*]

MATTIE. Run for the doctor, run for the doctor!

DOCTOR. I am Doctor Immanuel at your service, madam. [MATTIE *turns and glares at him a moment and slaps him in the face.* HENRY *snatches up the broom and begins chasing the doctor around the room and beating him. The doctor makes an effort to get his case and hat as he is pursued, calling out.*] This is wrong, wrong! Ye do not understand. [*He opens the door and flees into the night.* HENRY *falls into a chair and rocks back and forth, groaning and moaning.* MATTIE *comes sobbing up to him.*]

HENRY. [*Whirling and seizing* MATTIE *by the throat.*] Who are you? I know: Mattie. You sew for the heathen and worry your husband's life out about dirt. Now in the grave they'll be plenty of dirt. And you sing, and you sing; and you talk and you talk. [*He grabs the remaining bottle and uncorks it.*] Drink this here bottle o' stuff.

MATTIE. [*Clenching her teeth and fighting back.*] I won't, I won't! It'll poison me, it'll kill me!

HENRY. [*Pulling open her mouth and pouring the contents in.*] Nunh—unh, I reckin it won't! [*She swallows and coughs*

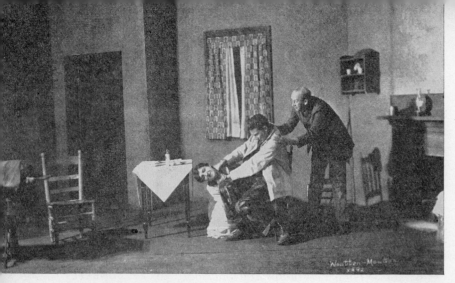

"I WON'T, I WON'T! IT'LL POISON ME, IT'LL KILL ME."

and strangles, then drops to the floor crying. HENRY *strides about the room kicking the furniture to pieces and throwing out his shoulders and shouting.*] I'm a new man, a man o' might, a he-man in Israel! [*Turning upon* MATTIE.] And you have drunk the drink. You gonna be humble down, a helpmate. [*He drops back in his chair in a dying posture.*]

MATTIE. Oh, Henry, Henry, baby!

HENRY. When I'm gone, take care of Pa. Let him live in peace. Let him have his tobacco and spet in the far. [MATTIE *crawls on her knees before him and lays her head in his lap, weeping.*]

MATTIE. Get the doctor, Father. Hitch up and go for the doctor. [*Old* JERNIGAN *starts for the door.* HENRY *jumps up and snatches him back.*]

HENRY. You ain't, you ain't. Let me die in peace. [*There is the sound of a medley of voices outside. Women gabbling in excitement.* MATTIE *climbs up to her feet and runs to the door.*]

MATTIE. Is that you, Mis' Bella? Come here, come here quick. Henry's poisoned and he's a-dying. [*The gabble and*

174

excitement outside increases. A voice replies from the yard.]

VOICE. I'm coming, Mattie, I'm coming. [*She is heard coming up on the steps.* HENRY *gets up from his chair and begins to bark like a dog, blubbering and growling.*]

HENRY. [*Shrieking again.*] I' been bit by a mad dog. [*He barks.*]

VOICE. Lord a-mercy, he's run mad! [*A low murmur of horror rises from the women outside, followed by shrieks and then the sound of running feet.* HENRY *rushes out of the door barking and pursuing them.*]

MATTIE. [*Looking at old* JERNIGAN *through her tears.*] He ain't been bit by no mad dog!

JERNIGAN. [*Stuttering with excitement.*] Mebbe that's the way the pizen works. That doctor said he got it a quare way in the middle of the night and a storm on and a' old man helping him.

MATTIE. He's crazy. [*Wringing her hands.*] Why'd you let him give Henry that stuff? The mess I took won't nothing, weak as water! [*She goes to the door calling piteously.*] Henry! Henry! [*Old* JERNIGAN *comes up to the bottle she has dropped and looks at it.*]

JERNIGAN. [*With a shout.*] He's tuk the wrong medicine, Mattie! He tuk that there gray stuff and you tuk the red!

MATTIE. [*At the door.*] Henry! Henry! [HENRY *comes back on the porch and gives a farewell bark.* MATTIE *runs out and throws her arms around him. He flings her from him and strides into the room. His shoes are covered with mud. He goes to the fireplace and stamps it off on the hearth.*]

JERNIGAN. [*Running up to him excitedly.*] Hyuh, hyuh, you tuk that gray stuff. Look, look!

HENRY. [*Waving him off.*] It don't make no difference. 'Twon't nothing but water. [MATTIE *comes in and stares at him as he casually cleans his boot on the hearth.*]

MATTIE. [*Whimpering.*] What's happened, Henry? You seem—

HENRY. I been cured, that's what. The medicine done it. [*He gets up, looks around the room, goes over to the machine, gathers up the clothes for the heathen, picks out a coat and trousers and throws them at the old man.*] Here, there's your Ransome Taylor coat and your britches. The heathen ain't gonna git 'em. [*He wipes his shoes with the other garments and then calmly goes to his chair and sits down.* MATTIE *has been looking on a moment and then with a glad cry of comprehension falls on her knees by him and lays her head sobbing in his lap.*]

JERNIGAN. [*Dropping in his chair thunderstruck.*] Well, I be durned if I ever seed the beat! [*He thinks a moment, and then bursts out in a low musical chuckle. His face spreads into a grin that breaks over his face in a thousand wrinkles. He cuts a caper on the floor, stopping now and then trying to comprehend what has happened.* HENRY *sits solemnly stroking* MATTIE's *head. The door is cracked open at the rear and* DOCTOR IMMANUEL *pokes his head in.*]

DOCTOR. Masters of this house—

HENRY. [*Turning and snarling.*] Hanh—Scat! [*He barks and the* DOCTOR *slams the door. After a moment* HENRY *calls old* JERNIGAN.] Pa, go and tell him to come in and get his hat and case. [MATTIE's *sobs gradually die away.*] Yeh, I know, poor child. I did scare you, didn't I? [*Only a whimper from* MATTIE *and hugging of* HENRY's *knees answered him.*]

JERNIGAN. [*At the door.*] Come on in, doctor, and get yer stuff. He ain't gonna hurt you. [*The* DOCTOR *comes gravely in and gets his case and hat.*]

HENRY. Pa, give him that five dollars.

JERNIGAN. [*His sides shaking with enjoyment.*] Hyuh,

hyuh, it is. You done it, Doc, same as you said you would.

HENRY. And you needn't come back. I don't need you!
[*He lifts his head with decision written on his face.*] Lemme
have a look at the plug of tobacco, Pa.

DOCTOR. [*At the door.*] Remember that I am always at
your service. Peace abide with you and this house always.
I am on my way now to another patient.

HENRY. That's all right, doctor. You needn't bother about
us. We ain't gonna need you no more. Are we, Mattie?

[MATTIE *shakes her head.*]

DOCTOR. [*Going out.*]

> As you all know, wherever I go,
> My name is Immanuel.

[*He closes the door and his chant dies away in the night.*]

HENRY. I said, Pa, I'd like a look at that tobacco.

MATTIE. [*Raising her head.*] Don't you spit on—

HENRY. [*Crushing her back on the floor.*] Nanh, nanh, I
tell you I been cured. I'm boss. [*Breaking into a loud roar-
ing laugh.*] Horray! Horray! I'm another man. I'm cured,
I'm boss. Gimme that 'backer. [*The old man hands it to
him eagerly.* HENRY *bites off an enormous chew and hands
the plug back. Old* JERNIGAN *hesitates a moment and then
also bites off a mouthful. A look of deep content comes over
him. He snuggles into a chair and chews.* HENRY *chews.
They look across at each other.* HENRY *signifies to the old
man with a motion of his hand that he spit first. Old* JERNI-
GAN *with signs refuses.* HENRY *spits profusely and loud in
the direction of the fire. Old* JERNIGAN *does likewise.*]

JERNIGAN. [*Eyeing* HENRY *slyly, as he rolls his tobacco
sweetly in his mouth.*] Hee—hee! [MATTIE *sits hugging*
HENRY's *knees.*]

HENRY. [*Nodding happily and wisely.*] Unh-hunh-yeh.

[*They sit saying nothing. Presently* HENRY *looks over at the old man and laughs suddenly and deeply.*]

JERNIGAN. What?

HENRY. I run them there women right into the mudhole out there.

JERNIGAN. [*Beating his thigh gleefully.*] Hee-hee! Hee-hee!

HENRY. I shore did. [*They lapse into silence. By this time* MATTIE *has somewhat raised her head and is staring contemplatively by* HENRY's *chin into the fire.*]

JERNIGAN. [*Shivering a bit and stirring the fire.*] Gonna be cold Henry, cold.

HENRY. Yeh.

JERNIGAN. Robins been flying towards the South all day. [*They both lean towards the fire and spit.*]

CURTAIN

RED DEATH

by

RUTH BARTH

This radio script narrates skillfully the heroic struggle of a doctor to discover the cause of a fatal disease which used to be common in the South: pellagra.

The writer, Ruth Barth, hails from Cedar Rapids, Iowa. When young she traveled to California where she studied in a girl's school, and then returned to Coe College in her native town. At first she wrote radio scripts for small stations in the West before she undertook to write for the major stations in New York. She is noted for her variety programs and a series which have been broadcast over CBS.

RED DEATH

[*Music.*]

NARRATOR. *The year 1915. The red soil of Georgia yields its rich rows of cotton. The hills and fields of America's southland are lush and green and the land is peaceful and good. The Gulf Coast is a blue curve against the high surf; and the rich sun slants through the canebrakes of the valley of the Mississippi. But stalking the Carolina hills, striding sure-footed across the copper earth of Georgia, through the black belt and beyond, is Death—a red and raging phantom. No man sees him; no man knows the time of his coming. For the Cropper's hoe will fall to the earth, and the man bend double with the agony inside him, and all men know it and the sure death it brings and the brand of doom it leaves on the faces of its victims—the mark of the Red Death —a mark shaped like a butterfly moth.*

[*Music up to a cut off.*]

[*Dog howl in distance.*]

[*Cabin door creaks open.*]

DR. HORNE. Well, Granny, I guess there's nothing more I can do here, now.

GRANNY. Dead. Sam's dead. They're all gone now. All my boys.

DR. HORNE. It's hard, I know. Hard for all of us, Granny.

GRANNY. Cotton's going to rot here this year—same as down to the Bennett's last year—when the misery took the old man away. Ain't this never goin' to let up, doctor?

DR. HORNE. All we can do is hope and pray, Granny.

[*Dog howl.*]

GRANNY. Hope and pray. What else I been doin', doctor?

181

DR. HORNE. [*with hope.*] I know, Granny, but maybe something will come of it. They say a big scientist is coming down here to find out what this sickness is.

GRANNY. I know what it is. It's the curse of the devil on poor folks.

DR. HORNE. Granny, sometimes, it seems like that's just what it is. But there must be a reason why, and maybe this man can help us. You see, he'll have laboratories and—ways of finding things out.

GRANNY. Maybe so. But that won't bring my boys back. Nothin'll bring them back to me.

[*Music up and down.*]

[*Out of music: train pulling out of station.*]

DR. HORNE. My name is Horne, Doctor Goldberger. Local practitioner here. Heard you were coming, and I wanted to be the first to meet you and the Missus.

GOLDBERGER. That's very kind of you, Dr. Horne.

DR. HORNE. Now, if there's anything I can do, you just have to ask me.

MARY. Well, we really ought to find a good boarding house someplace.

DR. HORNE. No—no. You'll do no such thing, ma'am. I want you to put up at my house 'til you're settled.

MARY. Oh, Dr. Horne, we wouldn't think of putting you to that trouble.

DR. HORNE. It'll be no trouble at all, ma'am. Besides, it'll give us a chance to get acquainted before we get the doctor an office for his laboratory.

GOLDBERGER. I have no laboratory, Dr. Horne.

DR. HORNE. You mean you didn't bring any equipment with you on the train?

GOLDBERGER. No. I mean I'm not going to have a laboratory. That is, what you think of as one.

DR. HORNE. Oh. Well, we've all done just about everything we can think of—but it's no use, I'm afraid. You're going to find out it's like trying to trap a ghost.

GOLDBERGER. I'll tell you, Dr. Horne. You ask me about a laboratory. These hills are my laboratory. I believe we'll never know anything about pellagra until we know these people . . . their habits . . . the way they live. I want to do that first.

DR. HORNE. Seems to me that's putting the cart before the horse. Not a thing about 'em I couldn't tell you right off. Why, if you'd just go over my case histories. . . .

GOLDBERGER. No. Thank you, Dr. Horne, but I don't think case histories will help. I believe the answer to this is the living. It's the lives these people live that must be studied. Not the deaths they die.

[*Music.*]

[*Horse and buggy effect.*]

GOLDBERGER. Whoa, there. Whoa! [*Buggy to halt.*]

ELMER. You—you lookin' for somebody hereabouts?

GOLDBERGER. No. No, I'm a stranger here. Thought I'd have a look around.

ELMER. Well, don't go near that cabin over there. They got the misery there bad.

GOLDBERGER. Oh? Friends of yours?

ELMER. They was. I don't go there no more. They're bad luck, those folks. They don't have *nothin'* but bad luck and it seems like the poorer they get the sicker they get.

GOLDBERGER. Oh! Isn't anyone looking after them?

ELMER. They can't afford no doctor. We'uns send over

what we can to eat. But we ain't got much ourselves.

GOLDBERGER. Maybe I could help them. I'm a doctor.

ELMER. You? You don't look like no doctor.

GOLDBERGER. Well, I'm a special kind.

ELMER. I sure hope you can fix up them folks over there.

GOLDBERGER. I'll do what I can.

ELMER. Say, doc . . .

GOLDBERGER. Yes?

ELMER. I don't want you to get the idea I got the misery. I ain't sick, mind you. It's just—I ain't feelin' so good.

GOLDBERGER. Let me look at the side of your face there. Seems to have a mark.

ELMER. Oh, that. That's sunburn. I get that every year, come spring.

GOLDBERGER. You get it in the spring, eh?

ELMER. Sure. Skin gets dry-like—from the sun. Like these here cracks between the knuckles. It don't hurt none.

GOLDBERGER. Let me see your hands.

ELMER. They don't hurt none, doc. It's like—like I'm so tired all the time. And there's a kind of a raw feelin' in my stomach sometimes—so I can't hardly eat.

GOLDBERGER. You—you sleep well?

ELMER. Tolerable. I don't hanker for too much sleep. I get bad dreams.

GOLDBERGER. I see.

ELMER. Doctor used to give a tonic like to the granny woman. Fixed her right up.

GOLDBERGER. Put her to sleep, you mean?

ELMER. Yeah. Doc, you don't think—

GOLDBERGER. We don't know much about this sickness,

lad. It may take us quite a while to find out what's causing it . . .

ELMER. Doc—you don't think I'm gettin' it, do you? Do you?

GOLDBERGER. Yes, son—I do. I'm afraid you've got it.

[*Music up and down.*]

NARRATOR. A mild-mannered, quiet-spoken doctor, following on the heels of the phantom Red Death; doing what he can along the way to help and comfort its victims. But the phantom itself is always just ahead of him, invincible and deadly. He quarantines houses, but the Red Death walks silently in past the guards. He isolates whole communities but the Red Death strikes as before. Once he thinks he has trapped it—in a test tube—yet he has only touched its shadow. But on he plods—in the footsteps of the Red Death. . . .

[*Music up to a cut-off.*]

[*Out of music: typing. Then paper rolled out of carrier.*]

MARY. There! It's finished.

GOLDBERGER. Thank you, dear. Looks very neat and impressive, doesn't it?

MARY. "The Etiology of Pellagra, by Joseph Goldberger." It sounds—so scientific, some way or other. Not like tramping along country roads and talking to all those people—not like you, Joseph.

GOLDBERGER. It has to be complicated or our friends on the commission wouldn't be able to understand it.

MARY. Joseph, it's amazing, when you think men have worked on this important problem for so long and the answer was as simple as this—

GOLDBERGER. You're right, Mary. It is simple. Just a month of balanced diet, of educating people against a restricted one of corn-meal, molasses and side-pork all the time. Do this and you'll end pellagra.

MARY. I wish I could be at the meeting to hear you.

GOLDBERGER. I wish you could too, Mary. I think we've proved our case.

[*Music.*]

[*Door opens and closes.*]

[*Steps on stairs.*]

MARY. [*Off.*] That you, Joseph?

GOLDBERGER. Yes, Mary.

MARY. [*Coming in.*] You've been gone so long!

GOLDBERGER. I had—an errand—at the hospital.

MARY. Joseph—what about the meeting—your report?

GOLDBERGER. They laughed at me.

MARY. Oh, no—they couldn't.

GOLDBERGER. They insisted in spite of all our evidence to the contrary—that a germ is causing pellagra. Why one jackass there—

MARY. Joseph!

GOLDBERGER. Well, he *was* a jackass. And I told him so—to his face.

MARY. I've never seen you angry like this before.

GOLDBERGER. Well, I am angry. An epidemic, like typhoid, he said . . . and they all nodded their heads, yes, a germ causes pellagra. Well, if it's laboratory work they want, they'll get it! I went down to the hospital this evening and got enough blood serum from pellagra victims to wipe out an army if pellagra were contagious.

MARY. What are you going to do?

GOLDBERGER. I'm going to inject it into my veins, my muscles and my spine . . . I'm going to smear it on my skin—to prove germs don't cause the disease.

MARY. I know how you feel, dear.

[*Pause.*] Joseph—

GOLDBERGER. Yes?

MARY. I am going to take the injections with you.

GOLDBERGER. Mary, I—

MARY. Two subjects for experiment would carry more weight than one.

GOLDBERGER. That has nothing to do with it.

MARY. Joseph, you and I have always been together. We've believed together. Shouldn't it be that way now?

GOLDBERGER. Mary—please!

MARY. There are some hypodermics here. And here's the alcohol—and cotton—[*Bottles clink.*] All right—I'm waiting. Please Joseph!

GOLDBERGER. Very well, Mary.

[*Pause.*]

MARY. There. Now, it's you. Roll up your sleeve, dear.

GOLDBERGER. Yes—there. All right, if they want this kind of proof—we'll give it to them.

[*Music up and down.*]

GOLDBERGER. Governor Brewer, I appreciate this opportunity to talk to you.

GOVERNOR. That's all right, Dr. Goldberger. Heard a lot about you. Did some work with Walter Reed in yellow fever, didn't you?

GOLDBERGER. Yes, sir. That was a great experience. Governor, I'm here to ask you a favor.

GOVERNOR. Sure man. Go ahead. What is it?

GOLDBERGER. I'd like to go into the State Penitentiary.

GOVERNOR. Well, there are a lot of laws you could break and get into prison, Dr. Goldberger.

GOLDBERGER. No—I want to conduct an experiment.

GOVERNOR. What kind of an experiment?

GOLDBERGER. Governor—I want to experiment with a group of convicts and induce pellagra.

GOVERNOR. What?

GOLDBERGER. Let me explain. Governor, I'm convinced pellagra is caused by the wrong kind of food. Not enough variety. Balance the diet and you will prevent pellagra.

GOVERNOR. I always heard it was caused by a germ.

GOLDBERGER. I know better. My wife and I injected ourselves with blood serum taken from dying pellagra victims. We did not contract it. I think that disposes of the germ theory.

GOVERNOR. Well, it doesn't prove a balanced diet will stop it.

GOLDBERGER. Right here in Jackson, Governor Brewer, I investigated pellagra cases in an orphange. I found out that children between six and twelve were fed on the typical poor family's rations of corn-meal and molasses, and most of them contracted pellagra.

GOVERNOR. Yes, I know about that.

GOLDBERGER. Then you ought to know about this, sir. Those that didn't have pellagra told me they were stealing milk and meat and vegetables on the sly. That meant they were getting a balanced diet. They warded off the disease that way.

GOVERNOR. Understand me, Dr. Goldberger, if I can help you get rid of this infernal plague, I'll do it. Now if I let you go over to the prison what would be your procedure?

GOLDBERGER. I will feed those convicts the average poor family's diet and they will develop pellagra.

GOVERNOR. But what if one of them dies? They'll call it cold-blooded murder.

GOLDBERGER. Those men won't die. I'll put them back on a balanced diet and it'll cure 'em.

GOVERNOR. You're sure you can?

GOLDBERGER. Yes, Governor, I am.

GOVERNOR. Then go ahead. I'll phone the Warden to pick out twelve men for you and you can give them your proposition.

GOLDBERGER. Thank you, Governor.

GOVERNOR. And, Goldberger, tell 'em this. If they're willing to take the risk, after it's over, I'll pardon each one.

GOLDBERGER. Governor Brewer—for this you'll have the gratitude of science and all humanity.

[*Music.*]

WARDEN. All right, boys, line up. [*Effect.*] Men—this is Dr. Goldberger. He's got something to say to you.

[*Murmurs—stir.*]

GOLDBERGER. Thank you, Warden. Men, I'll give you the good news first. If you'll do what is asked, the GOVERNOR will give each of you a pardon.

[*Violent reaction.*]

SAM. Doctor, Sir—you sure there ain't a catch in this somewhere?

GOLDBERGER. Yes. There *is* a catch in it. [*Stir.*] You will have to do just as I tell you. You will live in the new bunkhouse away from all the other prisoners. You'll get plenty to eat. You can stuff yourselves. I want you to. But all you'll get will be corn-bread, molasses, grits, side-pork and a few other things.

STEVE. Well, what are we waiting for?

GOLDBERGER. Not so fast. I still haven't come to the catch. And here it is. It is very possible that you will all contract a disease—pellagra.

[*Ad libs.*]

SAM. Excuse me, doctor, sir. But I know what that misery is. I seen my little sister die of it. Why you want to give anybody that kind of misery?

GOLDBERGER. Because if you men do contract pellagra, the world will know how to cure others who have it. We can drive it off the face of the earth.

JOE. I ain't goin' to get that misery for nobody!

[*Ad lib "Me neithers".*]

CHIMP. Aw, shut up. You-all want to get out of here, don't you? And maybe we won't catch it nohow.

STEVE. It's worth a chance.

JOE. I'll go, doctor.

[*Several ad lib "Me toos".*]

SAM. Doctor, you sure you can cure us up again if'n we catch it?

GOLDBERGER. I'm reasonably sure.

SAM. And we really get all the side-pork and corn-bread we can eat?

GOLDBERGER. That's right.

SAM. Then, I'm with you, too, doctor. And you tell the GOVERNOR he kin start gettin' ready with them pardons.

[*Music.*]

[*Instrument clink.*]

GOLDBERGER. All right—you may go now.

JOE. I'm on my way, doc.

[*Music.*]

[*Stir.*]

GOLDBERGER. Men, it's the last day of the experiment. Any complaints? Bring in 3216, doctor.

OWEN. [*Off.*] [*Door.*] 3216—come on in—the doctor's ready for you.

GOLDBERGER. Well, how *are* you feeling today?

STEVE. Never felt better.

GOLDBERGER. Sleep all right?

STEVE. Like a top.

GOLDBERGER. No pain anywhere?

STEVE. Nope.

OWEN. No marks on him anywhere, Dr. Goldberger.

GOLDBERGER. All right—you may go.

STEVE. [*Fading.*] Thanks.

[*Door close.*]

GOLDBERGER. I don't understand it. All this time and still not one case has developed. I've observed thousands of cases developing and primary symptoms should have appeared by now.

OWEN. There's still a man waiting outside. You want to examine him?

GOLDBERGER. Yes. Yes, we must complete the record.

OWEN. [*Going off.*] I'll call him in. [*Door open.*] 1430—

SAM. Yassuh.

OWEN. [*Off.*] You're next.

SAM. [*Coming in.*] Yassuh. I'm sure glad you decide to see me. It's near time for mess over to the bunkhouse—and I's hungry.

GOLDBERGER. I see—your appetite's all right, I take it.

SAM. Boy, do I feel good!

GOLDBERGER. Any sign, doctor?

OWEN. Not a single mark.

GOLDBERGER. Well, that settles it. I must be wrong—but I

don't see how I can be. This finishes me I— [*Door open.*] Yes, Warden?

WARDEN. You finished with this man?

GOLDBERGER. Yes. Yes, we're finished with all of 'em. The experiment has failed.

SAM. Doctor Goldberger, sir . . .

GOLDBERGER. Yes?

SAM. If'n you're leavin', I just want to thank you before you go—the pardon—and all that fine food—I appreciate it, indeed I do—

GOLDBERGER. That's all right.

SAM. And most especially that fine steak dinner.

GOLDBERGER. *Steak* dinner! Warden—what's this about a steak dinner?

WARDEN. Well, they was complainin' like about the same grub, doctor. And it bein' a holiday, I figured it wouldn't do 'em no harm.

GOLDBERGER. No harm! No wonder the experiment hasn't proved my point by now.

WARDEN. I didn't aim to interfere with your experiment. I just thought—

GOLDBERGER. Can't you understand what you've done? You've very nearly destroyed the one chance of finding the cause of pellagra. From now on, Warden, these men stick to the meals I prescribe. Is that clear?

WARDEN. Yes, sir. It won't happen again, sir.

[*Music.*]

[*Stir.*]

CHIMP. I tell ya, doc, I'm gettin' so I can't even stand the smell of corn-bread no more. Let's call it off and skip your supper tonight.

GOLDBERGER. We'd better look you all over again. Number 3216—

STEVE. [*Not very perkily.*] I'm feelin' okay, doc.

GOLDBERGER. You're sure?

STEVE. Yeah . . . Yeah, I'm sure. Well, maybe ate too much.

OWEN. No signs, Dr. Goldberger.

GOLDBERGER. Next. 1430—1430 . . .

SAM. I—I can't stand it no more. I—I—doc—I sure got the misery.

GOLDBERGER. Quick, examine this man.

SAM. I—my insides, doc— You gotta tell me if I got the misery. I—

OWEN. Dr. Goldberger! Look! Look here! Behind his ear.

GOLDBERGER. A red splotch! That's it! At last we've found it. Pellagra!

OWEN. Well, they can't laugh this time, doctor. This means the end of pellagra.

GOLDBERGER. No, this is only the beginning of the end. We've trapped our enemy. But we must defeat his allies— poverty and ignorance. And when we vanquish them, we will have finally vanquished pellagra.

[*Music.*]

NARRATOR. The red mark shaped like a butterfly moth. For years its brand meant death. But to a quiet, bespectacled doctor standing in a bunkhouse of a Mississippi State Prison it meant the climax of a long struggle; a struggle he has handed on to valiant men and women who today carry out his ideas, thus giving new hope to humanity. Through education, pellagra may well be vanquished in our lifetime. And for his ceaseless labor for the betterment of the human race, Doctor Joseph Goldberger joins the immortals.

[*Music up and finish.*]

ENTER THE HERO

by

THERESA HELBURN

This clever little satire, first produced by the St. Francis Little Theatre Players of San Francisco in 1918 pokes fun at a common adolescent trait. Too many young girls like to invent love scenes with acquaintances or strangers and act as if they were real. But when the hero enters, the dream world is likely to collapse.

Theresa Helburn was practically born to the theatre. From her early years she has been organizing, managing, and writing plays when not acting in them. In New York she has been the guiding genius and co-director of the Theatre Guild.

THERESA HELBURN
Co-director of Theatre Guild of New York City.

ENTER THE HERO

CHARACTERS

RUTH CAREY

ANNE CAREY

HAROLD   LAWSON

MRS. CAREY

The scene presents an upstairs sitting room in a comfortable house in a small city. The wall on the spectator's left is broken by a fireplace, and beyond that a door leading into the hall. At the back of the stage is a deep bay window from which one may have a view up and down the street. A door in the right wall leads to ANNE CAREY's *bedroom. The sitting room, being* ANNE's *particular property, is femininely furnished in chintz. A table desk with several drawers occupies an important place in the room, which is conspicuously rich in flowers.*

The curtain rises on an empty stage. RUTH CAREY, *a pretty girl of eighteen, enters hurriedly, carrying a large box; she wears a hat and coat.*

RUTH. Oh, Anne, here's *another* box of flowers! Anne, where are you?

VOICE. [*From* ANNE's *bedroom.*] In here. I thought you had gone out.

RUTH. [*Opening door left.*] I was just going when the expressman left these—and I wanted to see them. [*Looking into the bedroom.*] Oh, how pretty your dress is. Turn round. Just adorable! May I open these?

THE VOICE. Yes, but hurry. It's late.

RUTH. [*Throwing her sister a kiss.*] You dear! It's almost

197

like having a fiancé of my own. Three boxes in two days!
He's adorably extravagant. Oh, Anne, exquisite white roses!
Come, look!

[ANNE CAREY *appears in the bedroom door. She is a girl of
twenty-two. Her manner in this scene shows nervousness
and suppressed excitement.*]

ANNE. Yes, lovely. Get a bowl, Ruth. Quickly.

RUTH. I will. Here's a card. [*She hands* ANNE *an envelope,
goes to the door, then stops.*] What does he say, Anne? May
I see?

[ANNE, *who has read the card quickly with a curious
little smile, hands it back to her without turning.*]

RUTH. [*Reading.*]

> "The red rose whispers of passion
> And the white rose breathes of love;
> Oh, the red rose is a falcon,
> And the white rose is a dove.

> But I send you a cream-white rosebud
> With a flush on its petal tips,
> For the love that is purest and sweetest
> Has a kiss of desire on the lips."

Oh, how beautiful! Did he make that up, do you suppose?
I didn't know he was a real poet.

ANNE. [*Who has been pinning some of the roses on her
dress.*] Anyone in love is a poet.

RUTH. It's perfectly beautiful! [*She takes a pencil and
little notebook out of her pocket.*] May I copy it in my
"Harold Notebook"?

ANNE. Your *what?*

RUTH. I call it my "Harold Notebook." I've put down bits
of his letters that you read me, the lovely bits that are too

beautiful to forget. Do you mind?

ANNE. You silly child!

RUTH. Here, you may see it. . . . That's from the second letter he wrote you from Rio Janeiro. I just couldn't get over that letter. You know I made you read it to me three times. It was so—so delicate. I remembered this passage —see. "A young girl seems to me as exquisite and frail as a flower, and I feel myself a vandal in desiring to pluck and possess one. Yet, Anne, your face is always before me, and I know now what I was too stupid to realize before, that it was you and you only, who made life bearable for me last winter when I was a stranger and alone." Oh, Anne— [*Sighing rapturously.*] that's the sort of love letter I've dreamed of getting. I don't suppose I ever shall.

ANNE. [*Still looking over the notebook with her odd smile.*] Have you shown this to anyone?

RUTH. Only to Caroline—in confidence. [*Pauses to see how* ANNE *will take it.*] But really, Anne, everyone knows about Harold. You've told Madge and Eleanor, and I'm sure they've told the others. They don't say anything to us, but they do to Caroline and she tells me. [*Watching* ANNE'S *face.*] You're not angry, are you, Anne?

ANNE. Yes, rather. [*Then eagerly.*] What do they say?

RUTH. Oh, all sorts of things. Some of them horrid, of course! You can't blame them for being jealous. Here you are having just the sort of experience that any one of them would give their eye teeth to have. *I'd* be jealous if you weren't my sister. As it is, I seem to get some of the glory myself.

ANNE. [*Pleased, but disparaging.*] But every girl has this experience sooner or later.

RUTH. Oh, not in this way. Everything that Harold does

is beautiful, ideal. Jane Fenwick showed me some of Bob's letters. They were so dull, so prosaic! All about his salary and the corn crop. I was disgusted with them. So was she, I think, when she saw Harold's letters.

ANNE. Oh, you showed them to Jane too?

RUTH. [*A bit frightened.*] No, really I didn't. Caroline did. I lent her my notebook once overnight, and she gave Jane a peek—in the *strictest* confidence. Jane really needed it. She was getting so cocky about Bob. Girls are funny things, aren't they?

ANNE. [*Who has been keenly interested in all of Ruth's gossip.*] What do you mean?

RUTH. It isn't so much the man, as the idea of a man— someone to dream about, and to talk about. When I think of getting engaged—I suppose I shall get engaged some day —I never think of being really, really kissed by a man—

ANNE. What do you think of?

RUTH. I always think of telling Caroline about it, showing my ring to her and to Madge. Oh, Madge is green with envy. I believe she thought Harold sort of liked her. [ANNE *turns away.*] She was so excited when she saw him in New York. She said she would have got off the bus and chased him, but he went into a house. . . . Anne, why didn't you tell us—me, at least—that Harold was back from South America, before we heard it from Madge?

ANNE. Just because . . . I wanted to avoid all this . . . It was hard enough to have him within a few hours' distance and know he could not get to me. But it was easier when no one else knew. Don't you understand?

RUTH. Yes, dear, of course I do—but still—

ANNE. [*Impatiently.*] Now, Ruth, it's quarter past four. You promised—

RUTH. I'm going . . . right straight off . . . unless— Oh, Anne, mayn't I stay and have just one peek? I won't let him see me, and then I'll run straight away.

ANNE. Oh, for heaven's sake, don't be naughty and silly! Clear out now, quickly, or— [*Changing her tone suddenly.*] Ruth, dear, put yourself in my place. Think how you would feel if you were going to see the man you loved for the first time. That's what it really is. Think of it! Two years ago when he went away we were just the merest friends—and now—

RUTH. And now you're engaged to be married! Oh, isn't it the most romantic thing! Of course you want to be alone. Forgive me. Oh, Anne, how excited you must be!

ANNE. [*With rather histrionic intensity.*] No, I'm strangely calm. And yet, Ruth, I'm afraid, terribly afraid.

RUTH. Why, what of?

ANNE. [*Acting.*] I don't know . . . of everything . . . of the unknown. All this has been so wonderful, if anything should happen I don't think I could bear it. I think I should die.

RUTH. Nonsense, dear, what can happen? You're just on edge. Well, I'll be off. I'll join Mother at Aunt Nellie's. Give my love to Harold. You know I've never called him anything but Mr. Lawson to his face. Isn't that funny? Goodbye, dear. [*Throwing* ANNE *a kiss.*] You look so sweet.

ANNE. [*Her hands on* RUTH's *shoulder for an impressive moment.*] Goodbye, Ruth. Goodbye.

[*They kiss.*] [RUTH *goes. Left alone, a complete change comes over* ANNE. *She drops the romantic attitude. She is nervously determined. She quickly arranges the flowers, takes out the box, etc., straightens the room, and surveys herself rapidly in the mirror. There is a sound of wheels outside.*

ANNE *goes to the bay window and looks out. Then she stands erect in the grip of an emotion that is more like terror than anticipation. Hearing the sound of footsteps on the stair, she is panic-stricken and about to bolt, but at the sound of voices she pulls herself together and stands motionless.*]

MAN'S VOICE. [*Outside.*] In here? All right!

[HAROLD LAWSON *enters, a well set up, bronzed, rather commonplace young man of about twenty-eight. He sees no one on his entry, but as he advances into the room,* ANNE *comes down from the bay window.*]

HAROLD. Hello, Miss Carey, how are you? Splendid to see you again, after all this time. [ANNE *looks at him without speaking, which slightly embarrasses him.*] You're looking fine. How's your mother—and little Ruth?

ANNE. [*Slowly.*] Welcome home.

HAROLD. Oh, thanks. It's rather nice to be back in God's country. But it's not for long this time.

ANNE. Are you going away again?

HAROLD. Yes. I've another appointment. This one in India, some big salt mines. Not bad, eh? I made pretty good in Brazil, they tell me.

ANNE. [*Nervously.*] Sit down.

HAROLD. Thanks. Hot for September, isn't it? Though I ought to be used to heat by this time. Sometimes the thermometer would run a hundred and eight for a week on end. Not much fun, that.

ANNE. No, indeed.

HAROLD. [*Settling back comfortably to talk about himself.*] You know I loathed it down there at first. What with all the foreigners and the rotten weather and the bugs— thought I'd never get into the swing. Wanted to chuck engineering for any old job that was cool, but after a while—

ANNE. How long have you been home?

HAROLD. About three weeks. I'd really been meaning to come out here and have a look round my old haunts, but there was business in New York, and I had to go South and see my family—you know how time flies. Then your note came. It was mighty jolly of you to ask me out here. By the way, how did you know I was back?

ANNE. [*After a pause.*] Madge Kennedy caught sight of you in New York.

HAROLD. Did she really? How is little Madge? And that odd brother of hers. Is he just as much of a fool as ever? I remember once he said to me—

ANNE. Oh, I didn't ask you here to talk about Madge Kennedy's family.

HAROLD. [*Taken aback.*] No . . . no, of course not. I—er— I've been wondering just why you did ask me. You said you wanted to talk to me about something.

ANNE. [*Gently.*] Weren't you glad to come?

HAROLD. Why, of course I was. Of course. And then your note fired my curiosity—your asking me to come straight to you before seeing anyone else.

ANNE. Aren't you glad to be here with me?

HAROLD. Why, surely, of course, but— [*Pause.*]

ANNE. You see, people seemed to expect you would come to see me first of all. I rather expected it myself. Don't you understand?

HAROLD. [*Very uncomfortable.*] No . . . I'm afraid I don't . . .

ANNE. From the way you acted before you went away I thought you, yourself, would want to see me first of all.

HAROLD. Before I went away? What do you mean?

ANNE. You know well enough what I mean. The parties

those last weeks—the theater we went to—the beautiful flowers you sent Mother—the letter—

HAROLD. But—but—why, I was going away. You and your people had been awfully nice to me, a perfect stranger in town. I was simply trying to do the decent thing. Good Lord! You don't mean to say you thought—

ANNE. [*Watching him very closely.*] Yes, it's true, I thought—and everyone else thought—I've been waiting these two years for you to come back.

[*She drops her face into her hands. Her shoulders shake.*]

HAROLD. [*Jumping up.*] Great Heavens! I never imagined —Why, Miss Carey, I—oh, I'm terribly sorry! [*She continues to sob.*] Please don't do that—please! I'd better go away— I'll clear out—I'll go straight off to India—I'll never bother you again.

[*He has seized his hat, and is making, in a bewildered way, for the door, when she intercepts him.*]

ANNE. No. You mustn't go away!

HAROLD. But what can I do?

ANNE. [*Striking a tragic attitude.*] You mean to say you don't care at all—that you have never cared?

HAROLD. Really, Miss Carey, I—

ANNE. For heaven's sake, don't call me Miss Carey. Call me Anne.

HAROLD. Miss Carey . . . Anne . . . I . . . Oh, you'd better let me go—let me get away before anyone knows I'm here— before they think—

ANNE. It's too late. They think already.

HAROLD. Think what? What do you mean?

ANNE. Oh, this is terrible! Sit down, Harold, and listen to me. [*She pushes him into a chair and begins to talk very*

rapidly, watching intently the effect of her words upon him.]
You see, when you went away, people began to say things
about us—you and me—about your caring. I let them go on.
In fact I believed them. I suppose it was because I wanted
so much to believe them. Oh, what a fool I've been! What
a fool! [*She covers her face with her hands. He gets up, in-
tending vaguely to comfort her, but she thinks he is making
another move to go, and jumps to her feet.*] And now you
want to clear out like a thief in the night, and leave me to
be laughed at! No, no, you can't do that! You must help me.
You've hurt me to the very soul. You mustn't humiliate me
before the world.

HAROLD. I'll do anything I can, Miss Carey.

ANNE. Anne!

HAROLD. Anne, I mean. But how?

ANNE. [*After a moment's thought, as if the idea had just
come to her.*] You must stay here. You must pretend for a
few days—for a week at most, that we're engaged.

HAROLD. I can't do that, you know. Really, I can't.

ANNE. [*Going to him.*] Why not? Only a little while.
Then you'll go away to India. We'll find it's been a mistake.
I'll break it off,—it will only be a pretense, of course, but at
least no one will know what a fool I've been.

HAROLD. [*After a moment's hesitation.*] Miss Carey—Anne,
I mean, I'll do anything I can, but not that! A man can't do
that. You see, there's a girl, an English girl, down in Brazil,
I—

ANNE. Oh, a girl! Another! Well, after all, what does that
matter? Brazil is a long way off. She need never know.

HAROLD. She might hear. You can't keep things like this
hid. No. I wouldn't risk that. You'd better let me clear out
before your family gets home. No one need ever know I've
been here.

[*Again he makes a move toward the door.* ANNE *stands motionless.*]

ANNE. You can't go. You can't. It's more serious than you imagine.

HAROLD. Serious? What do you mean?

ANNE. Come here. [*He obeys. She sits in a big chair, but avoids looking at him. There is a delicate imitation of a tragic actress in the way she tells her story.*] I wonder if I can make you understand? It means so much to me that you should— so much! Harold, you know how dull life is here in this little town. You were glad enough to get away after a year of it, weren't you? Well, it's worse for a girl, with nothing to do but sit at home—and dream—of you. Yes, that's what I did, until, at last, when I couldn't stand it any longer, I wrote you.

HAROLD. [*Quickly.*] I never got the letter, Miss Carey. Honor bright, I didn't.

ANNE. Perhaps not, but you answered it.

HAROLD. Answered it? What are you talking about?

ANNE. Would you like to see your answer? [*She goes to the desk, takes a packet of letters out of a drawer, selects one, and hands it to him.*] Here it is—your answer. You see it's postmarked Rio Janeiro.

HAROLD. [*Takes it wonderingly.*] This does look like my writing. [*Reads.*] "Anne, my darling—" I say, what does this mean?

ANNE. Go on.

HAROLD. [*Reading.*] "I have your wonderful letter. It came to me like rain in the desert. Can it be true, Anne, that you do care? I ask myself a hundred times what I have done to deserve this. A young girl seems to me as exquisite and frail as a flower—" Great Scott! You don't think *I* could have written such stuff! What in the world!

ANNE. [*Handing over another letter.*] Here's the next letter you wrote me, from the mine. It's a beautiful one. Read it.

HAROLD. [*Tears it open angrily, and reads.*] "I have been out in the night under the stars. Oh, that you were here, my beloved! It is easy to stand the dust and the turmoil of the mine without you, but beauty that I cannot share with you hurts me like a pain—" [*He throws the letter on the table and turns toward her, speechless.*]

ANNE. [*Inexorably.*] Yes, that's an exceptionally beautiful one. But there are more—lots more. Would you like to see them?

HAROLD. But I tell you, I never wrote them. These aren't my letters.

ANNE. Whose are they, then?

HAROLD. [*Walking up and down furiously.*] God knows! This is some outrageous trick. You've been duped, you poor child. But we'll get to the bottom of this. Just leave it to me. I'll get detectives. I'll find out who's back of it! I'll—

[*He comes face to face with her and finds her looking quietly at him with something akin to critical interest.*]

HAROLD. Good Lord. What's the matter with me! You don't believe those letters. You couldn't think I wrote them, or you wouldn't have met me as you did, quite naturally, as an old friend. *You understand!* For heaven's sake, make it clear to me!

ANNE. I am trying to . . . I told you there had to be . . . answers . . . I was afraid to send my letters to you, but there had to be answers. [HAROLD *stares at her.*] So I wrote them myself.

HAROLD. You wrote them yourself?!?

ANNE. Yes.

HAROLD. These? These very letters?

ANNE. Yes. I had to.

HAROLD. Good God! [*He gazes at the litter of letters on the desk in stupefied silence.*] But the handwriting.

ANNE. Oh, that was easy. I had the letter you wrote to Mother.

HAROLD. And you learned to imitate my handwriting?

ANNE. [*Politely.*] It was very good writing.

HAROLD. [*In sudden apprehension.*] No one has seen these things,—have they?

ANNE. They arrived by mail.

HAROLD. You mean people saw the envelopes. Yes, that's bad enough . . . But you haven't shown them to anyone? [*At her silence, he turns furiously upon her.*] Have you? . . . Have you?

ANNE. [*Who enjoys her answer and its effect upon him.*] Only parts—never a whole letter. But it was such a pleasure to be able to talk about you to someone. My only pleasure.

HAROLD. Good heavens! You told people I wrote these letters? That we were engaged?

ANNE. I didn't mean to, Harold. Really, I didn't. But I couldn't keep it dark. There were your telegrams.

HAROLD. My telegrams? [*She goes to desk and produces a bundle of dispatches.*]

ANNE. [*Brazen in her sincerity.*] You used to wire me every time you changed your address. You were very thoughtful, Harold. But, of course, I couldn't keep those secret like your letters.

HAROLD. [*Standing helplessly, with the telegrams loose in his fingers.*] My telegrams! Good Lord! [*He opens one and reads.*] "Leaving Rio for fortnight of inspection in interior. Address care Señor Miguel—" *My* telegrams!

[*He flings the packet violently on the table, thereby almost upsetting a bowl of roses which he hastens to preserve.*]

ANNE. And then there were your flowers. I see you are admiring them. [*Harold withdraws as if the flowers were charged with electricity.*]

HAROLD. What flowers?

ANNE. These—these—all of them. You sent me flowers every week while you were gone.

HAROLD. [*Overcome.*] Good God! [*He has now reached the apex of his amazement and becomes sardonic.*]

ANNE. Yes. You were extravagant with flowers, Harold. Of course I love them, but I had to scold you about spending so much money.

HAROLD. Spending so much money? And what did I say when you scolded me?

ANNE. [*Taken aback only for a moment by his changed attitude.*] You sent me a bigger bunch than ever before—and—wait a minute—here's the card you put in it. [*She goes to the same fatal desk and produces a package of florist's cards.*]

HAROLD. Are all those my cards too?

ANNE. Yes.

HAROLD. [*Laughing a bit wildly.*] I'm afraid I *was* a bit extravagant!

ANNE. Here's the one! You wrote: "If all that I have, and all that I am, is too little to lay before you, how can these poor flowers be much?"

HAROLD. I wrote that? Very pretty—very. I'd forgotten I had any such knack at sentiments.

ANNE. And then, right away, you sent me the ring.

HAROLD. [*Jumps, startled out of his sardonic pose.*] Ring! What ring?

ANNE. My engagement ring. You really were very extravagant that time, Harold.

HAROLD. [*Looking fearfully at her hands.*] But I don't see . . . You're not wearing . . . ?

ANNE. Not there—here, next to my heart. [*She takes out a ring which hangs on a chain inside her frock, and presses it to her lips. Looking at him ·deeply.*] I adore sapphires, Harold. [*A new fear comes into* HAROLD'S *eyes. He begins to humor her.*]

HAROLD. Yes. Yes. Of course. Everyone likes sapphires, Anne. It is a beauty. Yes. [*He comes very close to her, and speaks very gently, as if to a child.*] You haven't shown your ring to anyone, have you, Anne?

ANNE. Only to a few people—one or two.

HAROLD. A few people! Good heavens! [*Then he controls himself, takes her hands gently in his, and continues speaking, as if to a child.*] Sit down, Anne; we must talk this over a little,—very quietly, you understand, very quietly. Now to begin with, when did you first—

ANNE. [*Breaks away from him with a little laugh.*] No, I'm not crazy. Don't be worried. I'm perfectly sane. I had to tell you all this to show how serious it was. Now you know. What are you going to do?

HAROLD. Do? [*He slowly straightens up as if the knowledge of her sanity had relieved him of a heavy load.*] I'm going to take the next train back to New York.

ANNE. And leave me to get out of this before people all alone?

HAROLD. You got into it without my assistance, didn't you? Great Scott, you forged those letters in cold blood—

ANNE. Not in cold blood, Harold. Remember, I cared.

HAROLD. I don't believe it. [*Accusingly.*] You enjoyed writing those letters!

ANNE. Of course I enjoyed it. It meant thinking of you, talking of—

HAROLD. Rot! Not of me, really. You don't think I am really the sort of person who could write that—that drivel!

ANNE. [*Hurt.*] Oh, I don't know. After a while I suppose you and my dream got confused.

HAROLD. But it was the rankest—

ANNE. Oh, I'm not so different from other girls. We're all like that. [*Repeating* RUTH's *phrase reminiscently.*] We must have someone to dream about—to talk about. I suppose it's because we haven't enough to do. And then we don't have any—any real adventures like—shop girls.

HAROLD. [*Surprised at this bit of reality.*] That's a funny thing to say!

ANNE. Well, it's true. I know I went rather far. After I got started I couldn't stop. I didn't want to, either. It took hold of me. So I went on and on and let people think whatever they wanted. But if you go now and people find out what I've done, they'll think I'm really mad—or something worse. Life will be impossible for me here, don't you see— impossible. [HAROLD *is silent.*] But if you stay, it will be so easy. Just a day or two. Then you will have to go to India. Is that much to ask? [*Acting.*] And you save me from disgrace, from ruin! [HAROLD *remains silent, troubled.*]

ANNE. [*Becoming impassioned.*] You must help me. You *must*. After I've been so frank with you, you can't go back on me now. I've never in my life talked to anyone like this —so openly. You *can't* go back on me! If you leave me here to be laughed at, mocked at by everyone, I don't know what I shall do. I shan't be responsible. If you have any kindness,

and chivalry . . . Oh, for God's sake, Harold, help me, help
me! [*Kneels at his feet.*]

HAROLD. I don't know . . . I'm horribly muddled . . . All
right, I'll stay!

ANNE. Good! Good! Oh, you are fine! I knew you would
be. Now everything will be so simple. [*The vista opens
before her.*] We will be very quiet here for a couple of days.
We won't see many people, for of course it isn't announced.
And then you will go . . . and I will write you a letter . . .

HAROLD. [*Disagreeably struck by the phrase.*] Write me
a letter? What for?

ANNE. [*Ingenuously.*] Telling you that I have been mistaken. Releasing you from the engagement . . . and you will
write me an answer . . . sad but manly . . . reluctantly accept-
ing my decision . . .

HAROLD. Oh, I am to write an answer, sad but manly—
Good God! Suppose you don't release me after all!

ANNE. Don't be silly, Harold. I promise. Can't you trust
me?

HAROLD. Trust you?

[*His eyes travel quickly from the table littered with letters
and dispatches to the flowers that ornament the room, back
to the table and finally to the ring that now hangs conspicuously on her breast. She follows the look and instinctively puts her hand to the ring.*]

Trust you? By Jove, no, I don't trust you! This is absurd.
I don't stay another moment. Say what you will to people.
I'm off. This is final.

ANNE. [*Who has stepped to the window.*] You can't go
now. I hear Mother and Ruth coming.

HAROLD. All the more reason.

[*He finds his hat.*]

I bolt.

ANNE. [*Blocking the door.*] You can't go, Harold! Don't corner me. I'll fight like a wildcat if you do.

HAROLD. Fight?

ANNE. Yes. A pretty figure you'll cut if you bolt now. They'll think you a cad—an out and out cad! Haven't they seen your letters come week by week, and your presents? And you have written to Mother, too—I have your letter. There won't be anything bad enough to say about you. They'll say you jilted me for that English girl in Brazil. It will be true, too. And it will get about. She'll hear of it, I'll see to that—and then—

HAROLD. But it's a complete lie! I can explain—

ANNE. You'll have a hard time explaining your letters and your presents—and your ring. There's a deal of evidence against you—

HAROLD. See here, are you trying to blackmail me? Oh, this is too ridiculous!

ANNE. They're coming! I hear them on the stairs! What are you going to tell them?

HAROLD. The truth. I must get clear of all this. I tell you—

ANNE. [*Suddenly clinging to him.*] No, no, Harold! Forgive me, I was just testing you. I will get you out of this. Leave it to me.

HAROLD. [*Struggling with her.*] No, I won't leave anything to you, *ever.*

ANNE. [*Still clinging tightly.*] Harold, remember I am a woman—and I love you.

[*This brings him up short a moment to wonder, and in this moment there is a knock at the door.*]

ANNE. [*Abandoning* HAROLD.] Come in.

[*There is a discreet pause.*]

MRS. CAREY'S VOICE. [*Off stage.*] May we come in?

ANNE. [*Angrily.*] Yes!

[HAROLD, *who has moved toward the door, meets* MRS. CAREY *as she enters. She throws her arms about his neck and kisses him warmly. She is followed by* RUTH.]

MRS. CAREY. Harold! My dear boy!

RUTH. [*Clutching his arm.*] Hello, Harold. I am so glad.

[HAROLD, *temporarily overwhelmed by the onslaught of the two women, is about to speak, when* ANNE *interrupts dramatically.*]

ANNE. Wait a moment, Mother. Before you say anything more I must tell you that Harold and I are no longer engaged!

[MRS. CAREY *and* RUTH *draw away from* HAROLD *in horror-struck surprise.*]

MRS. CAREY. No longer engaged? Why . . . What . . . ?

HAROLD. Really, Mrs. Carey, I—

ANNE. [*Interrupts, going to her mother.*] Mother, dear, be patient with me, trust me, I beg of you—and please, please don't ask me any questions. Harold and I have had a very hard—a very painful hour together. I don't think I can stand any more.

[*She is visibly very much exhausted, gasping for breath.*]

MRS. CAREY. Oh, my poor child, what is it? What has he done?

[*She supports* ANNE *on one side while* RUTH *hurries to the other.*]

HAROLD. Really, Mrs. Carey, I think I can explain.

ANNE. No, Harold, there's no use trying to explain. There are some things a woman feels, about which she cannot reason. I know I am doing right.

HAROLD. [*Desperately.*] Mrs. Carey, I assure you—

ANNE. [*As if on the verge of a nervous crisis.*] Oh, please, *please*, Harold, don't protest any more. I am not blaming you. Understand, Mother, I am not blaming him. But my decision is irrevocable. I thought you understood. I beg you to go away. You have just time to catch the afternoon express.

HAROLD. Nonsense, Anne, you must let me—

ANNE. [*Wildly.*] No, no, Harold, it is finished! Don't you understand? Finished!

[*She abandons the support of her mother and* RUTH *and goes to the table.*]

See, here are your letters. I am going to burn them.

[*She throws the packet into the fire.*]

All your letters—

[*She throws the dispatches into the fire.*]

Don't, please, continue this unendurable situation any longer. Go, I beg of you, go!

[*She is almost hysterical.*]

HAROLD. But I tell you I must—

ANNE. [*Falling back in her mother's arms.*] Make him go, Mother! Make him go!

MRS. CAREY. Yes, go! Go, sir! Don't you see you are torturing the child. I insist upon your going.

RUTH. Yes, she is in a dreadful state.

[*Here* MRS. CAREY *and* RUTH *fall into simultaneous urgings.*]

HAROLD. [*Who has tried in vain to make himself heard.*] All right, I'm going, I give up!

[*He seizes his hat and rushes out, banging the door behind him.* ANNE *breaks away from her mother and sister, totters rapidly to the door and calls down gently.*]

ANNE. Not in anger, I beg of you, Harold! I am not blaming you. Good-bye.

[*The street door is heard to bang.* ANNE *collapses in approved tragedy style.*]

ANNE. [*Gasping.*] Get some water, Ruth. I shall be all right in a moment.

[RUTH *rushes into the bedroom.*]

MRS. CAREY. Oh, my dear child, calm yourself. Mother is here, dear. She will take care of you. Tell me, dear, tell me.

[RUTH *returns with the water.* ANNE *sips a little.*]

ANNE. I will, mother—I will . . . everything . . . later. [*She drinks.*] But now I must be alone. Please, dear, go away . . . for a little while. I must be alone [*Rising and moving to the fire.*] with the ruin of my dreams.

[*She puts her arms on the chimney shelf and drops her head on them.*]

RUTH. Come, Mother! Come away!

MRS. CAREY. Yes, I am coming. We shall be in the next room, Anne, when you want us. Right here.

ANNE. [*As they go out, raises her head and murmurs.*] Dust and ashes! Dust and ashes!

[*As soon as they have gone,* ANNE *straightens up slowly. She pulls herself together after the physical strain of her acting. Then she looks at the watch on her wrist and sighs a long triumphant sigh. Her eye falls on the desk and she sees the package of florist's cards still there. She picks them up, returns with them to the fire and is about to throw them in, when her eye is caught by the writing on one. She takes it out and reads it. Then she takes another—and another. She stops and looks away dreamily. Then slowly, she moves back to the desk, drops the cards into a drawer and locks it.*]

She sits brooding at the desk and the open paper before her seems to fascinate her. As if in a dream she picks up a pencil. A creative look comes into her eyes. Resting her chin on her left hand, she begins slowly to write, murmuring to herself.]

ANNE. [*Reading as she writes.*] "Anne, my dearest . . .I am on the train . . . broken, shattered . . . Why have you done this to me . . . why have you darkened the sun . . . and put out the stars . . . put out the stars . . . Give me another chance, Anne . . . I will make good . . . I promise you . . . For God's sake, Anne, don't shut me out of your life utterly . . . I cannot bear it. . . . I . . ."

THE CURTAIN

has fallen slowly as she writes.

A SUNNY MORNING

by

QUINTERO BROTHERS

English text by LUCRETIA XAVIER FLOYD

Sunny and fragrant as the Andalusia of southern Spain is the international popular playlet here presented. Wit, sentiment, and good humor breathe from the pages of the play.

The brother-playwrights, Serafín and Joaquín Alvarez Quintero, began writing short farces known as *sainetes* followed by 150 long plays. These mainly treat of the customs and manners of the Andalusian folk. A number of them have been translated into other languages. Most popular in the English-speaking world have been *Fortunato, The Lady from Alfaqueque, A Hundred Years Old,* and *The Women Have Their Way.*

SERAFIN Y JOAQUIN ALVAREZ QUINTERO
BROTHER-PLAYWRIGHTS OF THE SPANISH STAGE.

A SUNNY MORNING

CHARACTERS

DOÑA LAURA
PETRA, *her maid*
DON GONZALO
JUANITA, *his servant*

SCENE: *A retired corner in a Park in Madrid.*
TIME: *The present.*

SCENE: *A sunny morning in a retired corner of a park in Madrid. Autumn. A bench at Right.* DOÑA LAURA, *a handsome, white-haired old lady of about seventy, refined in appearance, her bright eyes and entire manner giving evidence that despite her age her mental faculties are unimpaired, enters leaning upon the arm of her maid,* PETRA. *In her free hand she carries a parasol, which serves also as a cane.*

DOÑA LAURA. I am so glad to be here. I feared my seat would be occupied. What a beautiful morning!

PETRA. The sun is hot.

DOÑA LAURA. Yes, you are only twenty. [*She sits down on the bench.*] Oh, I feel more tired today than usual. [*Noticing* PETRA, *who seems impatient.*] Go, if you wish to chat with your guard.

PETRA. He is not mine, senora; he belongs to the park.

DOÑA LAURA. He belongs more to you than he does to the park. Go find him, but remain within calling distance.

PETRA. I see him over there waiting for me.

DOÑA LAURA. Do not remain more than ten minutes.

221

PETER. Very well, señora.   [*Walks toward* R.]

DOÑA LAURA. Wait a moment.

PETER. What does the señora wish?

DOÑA LAURA. Give me the bread crumbs.

PETRA. I don't know what is the matter with me.

DOÑA LAURA. [*Smiling.*] I do. Your head is where your heart is—with the guard.

PETER. Here, señora. [*She hands* DOÑA LAURA *a small bag. Exit* PETRA *by* R.]

DOÑA LAURA. Adios. [*Glances toward trees at* R.] Here they come! They know just when to expect me. [*She rises, walks toward* R., *and throws three handfuls of bread crumbs.*] These are for the spryest, these for the gluttons, and these for the little ones which are the most persistent. [*Laughs. She returns to her seat and watches, with a pleased expression, the pigeons feeding.*] There, that big one is always first! I know him by his big head. Now one, now another, now two, now three—— That little fellow is the least timid. I believe he would eat from my hand. That one takes his piece and flies up to that branch alone. He is a philosopher. But where do they all come from? It seems as if the news had spread. Ha, ha! Don't quarrel. There is enough for all. I'll bring more tomorrow.

[*Enter* DON GONZALO *and* JUANITO *from* L.C. DON GONZALO *is an old gentleman of seventy, gouty and impatient. He leans upon* JUANITO's *arm and drags his feet somewhat as he walks.*]

DON GONZALO. Idling their time away! They should be saying mass.

JUANITA. You can sit here, señor. There is only a lady. [DOÑA LAURA *turns her head and listens.*]

DON GONZALO. I won't, Juanito. I want a bench to myself.

JUANITO. But there is none.

DON GONZALO. That one over there is mine.

JUANITO. There are three priests sitting there.

DON GONZALO. Rout them out. Have they gone?

JUANITO. No, indeed. They are talking.

DON GONZALO. Just as if they were glued to the seat. No hope of their leaving. Come this way, Juanito. [*They walk toward the birds, Right.*]

DOÑA LAURA. [*Indignantly.*] Look out!

DON GONZALO. Are you speaking to me, senora?

DOÑA LAURA. Yes, to you.

DON GONZALO. What do you wish?

DOÑA LAURA. You have scared away the birds who were feeding on my crumbs.

DON GONZALO. What do I care about the birds?

DOÑA LAURA. But I do.

DON GONZALO. This is a public park.

DOÑA LAURA. Then why do you complain that the priests have taken your bench?

DON GONZALO. Señora, we have not met. I cannot imagine why you take the liberty of addressing me. Come, Juanito. [BOTH *go out* R.]

DOÑA LAURA. What an ill-natured old man! Why must people get so fussy and cross when they reach a certain age? [*Looking toward* R.] I am glad. He lost that bench, too. Serves him right for scaring the birds. He is furious. Yes, yes; find a seat if you can. Poor man! He is wiping the perspiration from his face. Here he comes. A carriage would not raise more dust than his feet. [*Enter* DON GONZALO *and* JUANITO *by* R. *and walk toward* L.]

DON GONZALO. Have the priests gone yet, Juanito?

JUANITO. No, indeed, senor. They are still there.

DON GONZALO. The authorities should place more benches here for these sunny mornings. Well, I suppose I must resign myself and sit on the bench with the old lady. [*Muttering to himself, he sits at the extreme end of* DOÑA LAURA'S *bench and looks at her indignantly. Touches his hat as he greets her.*] Good morning.

DOÑA LAURA. What you here again?

DON GONZALO. I repeat that we have not met.

DOÑA LAURA. I was responding to your salute.

DON GONZALO. "Good morning" should be answered by "good morning," and that is all you should have said.

DOÑA LAURA. You should have asked permission to sit on this bench, which is mine.

DON GONZALO. The benches here are public property.

DOÑA LAURA. Why, you said the one the priests have was yours.

DON GONZALO. Very well, very well. I have nothing more to say. [*Between his teeth.*] Senile old lady! She ought to be at home knitting and counting her beads.

DOÑA LAURA. Don't grumble any more. I'm not going to leave just to please you.

DON GONZALO. [*Brushing the dust from his shoes with his handkerchief.*] If the ground were sprinkled a little it would be an improvement.

DOÑA LAURA. Do you use your handkerchief as a shoe brush?

DON GONZALO. Why not?

DOÑA LAURA. Do you use a shoe brush as a handkerchief?

DON GONZALO. What right have you to criticize my actions?

DOÑA LAURA. A neighbor's right.

DON GONZALO. Juanito, my book. I do not care to listen to nonsense.

DOÑA LAURA. You are very polite.

DON GONZALO. Pardon me, señora, but never interfere with what does not concern you.

DOÑA LAURA. I generally say what I think.

DON GONZALO. And more to the same effect. Give me the book, Juanito.

JUANITO. Here, señor. [JUANITO *takes a book from his pocket, hands it to* DON GONZALO, *then exits by* R. DON GONZALO, *casting indignant glances at* DOÑA LAURA, *puts on an enormous pair of glasses, takes from his pocket a reading-glass, adjusts both to suit him, and opens his book.*]

DOÑA LAURA. I thought you were taking out a telescope.

DON GONZALO. Was that you?

DOÑA LAURA. Your sight must be keen.

DON GONZALO. Keener than yours is.

DOÑA LAURA. Yes, evidently.

DON GONZALO. Ask the hares and partridges.

DOÑA LAURA. Ah! Do you hunt?

DON GONZALO. I did, and even now——

DOÑA LAURA. Oh, yes, of course!

DON GONZALO. Yes, señora. Every Sunday I take my gun and dog, you understand, and go to one of my estates near Aravaca and kill time.

DOÑA LAURA. Yes, kill time. That is all you kill.

DON GONZALO. Do you think so? I could show you a wild boar's head in my study——

DOÑA LAURA. Yes, and I could show you a tiger's skin in my boudoir. What does that prove?

DON GONZALO. Very well, señora, please allow me to read. Enough conversation.

DOÑA LAURA. Well, you subside, then.

DON GONZALO. But first I shall take a pinch of snuff. [*Takes out snuff box.*] Will you have some? [*Offers box to* DOÑA LAURA.]

DOÑA LAURA. If it is good.

DON GONZALO. It is of the finest. You will like it.

DOÑA LAURA. [*Taking pinch of snuff.*] It clears my head.

DON GONZALO. And mine.

DOÑA LAURA. Do you sneeze?

DON GONZALO. Yes, señora, three times.

DOÑA LAURA. And so do I. What a coincidence!

[*After taking the snuff, they await the sneezes, both anxiously, and sneeze alternately three times each.*]

DON GONZALO. There, I feel better.

DOÑA LAURA. So do I. [*Aside.*] The snuff has made peace between us.

DON GONZALO. You will excuse me if I read aloud?

DOÑA LAURA. Read as loud as you please; you will not disturb me.

DON GONZALO. [*Reading.*] "All love is sad, but sad as it is, it is the best thing that we know." That is from Campoamor.

DOÑA LAURA. Ah!

DON GONZALO. [*Reading.*] "The daughters of the mothers I once loved kiss me now as they would a graven image." Those lines, I take it, are in a humorous vein.

DOÑA LAURA. [*Laughing.*] I take them so, too.

DON GONZALO. There are some beautiful poems in this book. Here. "Twenty years pass. He returns."

DOÑA LAURA. You cannot imagine how it affects me to see you reading with all those glasses.

DON GONZALO. Can you read without any?

DOÑA LAURA. Certainly.

DON GONZALO. At your age? You're jesting.

DOÑA LAURA. Pass me the book, then. [*Takes book; reads aloud.*]

> "Twenty years pass. He returns.
> And each, beholding the other, exclaims—
> Can it be that this is he?
> Heavens, is it she?".

[DOÑA LAURA *returns the book to* DON GONZALO.]

DON GONZALO. Indeed, I envy you your wonderful eyesight.

DOÑA LAURA. [*Aside.*] I know every word by heart.

DON GONZALO. I am very fond of good verses, very fond. I even composed some in my youth.

DOÑA LAURA. Good ones?

DON GONZALO. Of all kinds. I was a great friend of Espronceda, Zorilla, Bécquer, and others. I first met Zorilla in America.

DOÑA LAURA. Why, have you been in America?

DON GONZALO. Several times. The first time I went I was only six years old.

DOÑA LAURA. You must have gone with Columbus in one of his caravels!

DON GONZALO. [*Laughing.*] Not quite as bad as that. I am old, I admit, but I did not know Ferdinand and Isabella. [*They both laugh.*] I was also a great friend of Campoamor. I met him in Valencia. I am a native of that city.

DOÑA LAURA. You are?

DON GONZALO. I was brought up there and there I spent my early youth. Have you ever visited that city?

DOÑA LAURA. Yes, señor. Not far from Valencia there was a villa that, if still there, should retain memories of me. I spent several seasons there. It was many, many years ago.

It was near the sea, hidden away among lemon and orange trees. They called it—let me see, what did they call it— Maricela.

DON GONZALO. [*Startled.*] Maricela?

DOÑA LAURA. Maricela. Is the name familiar to you?

DON GONZALO. Yes, very familiar. If my memory serves me right, for we forget as we grow old, there lived in that villa the most beautiful woman I have ever seen, and I assure you I have seen many. Let me see—what was her name? Laura—Laura—Laura Llorente.

DOÑA LAURA. [*Standing.*] Laura Llorente?

DON GONZALO. Yes. [*They look at each other intently.*]

DOÑA LAURA. [*Recovering herself.*] Nothing. You remind me of my best friend.

DON GONZALO. How strange!

DOÑA LAURA. It is strange. She was called "The Silver Maiden."

DON GONZALO. Precisely, "The Silver Maiden." By that name she was known in that locality. I seem to see her as if she were before me now, at that window with the red roses. Do you remember that window?

DOÑA LAURA. Yes, I remember. It was the window of her room.

DON GONZALO. She spent many hours there. I mean in my day.

DOÑA LAURA. [*Sighing.*] And in mine, too.

DON GONZALO. She was ideal. Fair as a lily, jet black hair and black eyes, with an uncommonly sweet expression. She seemed to cast a radiance wherever she was. Her figure was beautiful, perfect. "What forms of sovereign beauty God models in human clay!" She was a dream.

DOÑA LAURA. [*Aside.*] If you but knew that dream was

now by your side, you would realize what dreams come to. [*Aloud.*] She was very unfortunate and had a sad love affair.

DON GONZALO. Very sad. [*They look at each other.*]

DOÑA LAURA. Did you hear of it?

DON GONZALO. Yes.

DOÑA LAURA. The ways of Providence are strange. [*Aside.*] Gonzalo!

DON GONZALO. The gallant lover, in the same affair——

DOÑA LAURA. Ah, the duel?

DON GONZALO. Precisely, the duel. The gallant lover was —my cousin, of whom I was very fond.

DOÑA LAURA. Oh, yes, a cousin? My friend told me in one of her letters the story of that affair, which was truly romantic. He, your cousin, passed by on horseback every morning down the rose path under her window, and tossed up to her balcony a bouquet of flowers which she caught.

DON GONZALO. And later in the afternoon the gallant horseman would return by the same path, and catch the bouquet of flowers she would toss him. Am I right?

DOÑA LAURA. Yes. They wanted to marry her to a merchant whom she would not have.

DON GONZALO. And one night, when my cousin waited under her window to hear her sing, this other person presented himself unexpectedly.

DOÑA LAURA. And insulted your cousin.

DON GONZALO. There was a quarrel.

DOÑA LAURA. And later a duel.

DON GONZALO. Yes, at sunrise, on the beach, and the merchant was badly wounded. My cousin had to conceal himself for a few days and later to fly.

DOÑA LAURA. You seem to know the story well.

DON GONZALO. And so do you.

DOÑA LAURA. I have explained that a friend repeated it to me.

DON GONZALO. As my cousin did to me. [*Aside.*] This is Laura!

DOÑA LAURA. [*Aside.*] Why tell him? He does not suspect.

DON GONZALO. [*Aside.*] She is entirely innocent.

DOÑA LAURA. And was it you, by any chance, who advised your cousin to forget Laura?

DON GONZALO. Why, my cousin never forgot her!

DOÑA LAURA. How do you account, then, for his conduct?

DON GONZALO. I will tell you. The young man took refuge in my house, fearful of the consequences of a duel with a person highly regarded in that locality. From my home he went to Seville, then came to Madrid. He wrote Laura many letters, some of them in verse. But undoubtedly they were intercepted by her parents, for she never answered at all. Gonzalo then, in despair, believing his love lost to him forever, joined the army, went to Africa, and there, in a trench, met a glorious death, grasping the flag of Spain and whispering the name of his beloved Laura——

DOÑA LAURA. [*Aside.*] What an atrocious lie!

DON GONZALO. [*Aside.*] I could not have killed myself more gloriously.

DOÑA LAURA. You must have been prostrated by the calamity.

DON GONZALO. Yes, indeed, señora. As if he were my brother. I presume, though, on the contrary, that Laura in a short time was chasing butterflies in her garden, indifferent to regret.

DOÑA LAURA. No, señor, no!

DON GONZALO. It is woman's way.

DOÑA LAURA. Even if it were woman's way, "The Silver Maiden" was not of that disposition. My friend awaited news for days, months, a year, and no letter came. One afternoon, just at sunset, as the first stars were appearing, she was seen to leave the house, and with quickening steps wend her way toward the beach, the beach where her beloved had risked his life. She wrote his name on the sand, then sat down upon a rock, her gaze fixed upon the horizon. The waves murmured their eternal threnody° and slowly crept up to the rock where the maiden sat. The tide rose with a boom and swept her out to sea.

DON GONZALO. Good heavens!

DOÑA LAURA. The fishermen of that shore who often tell the story affirm that it was a long time before the waves washed away that name written on the sand. [*Aside.*] You will not get ahead of me in decorating my own funeral.

DON GONZALO. [*Aside.*] She lies worse than I do.

DOÑA LAURA. Poor Laura!

DON GONZALO. Poor Gonzalo!

DOÑA LAURA. [*Aside.*] I will not tell him that I married two years later.

DON GONZALO. [*Aside.*] In three months I ran off to Paris with a ballet dancer.

DOÑA LAURA. Fate is curious. Here are you and I, complete strangers, met by chance, discussing the romance of old friends of long ago! We have been conversing as if we were old friends.

DON GONZALO. Yet, it is curious, considering the ill-natured prelude to our conversation.

DOÑA LAURA. You scared away the birds.

DON GONZALO. I was unreasonable, perhaps.

° A funeral song.

DOÑA LAURA. Yes, that was evident. [*Sweetly.*] Are you coming again tomorrow?

DON GONZALO. Most certainly, if it is a sunny morning. And not only will I not scare away the birds, but I will bring a few crumbs.

DOÑA LAURA. Thank you very much. Birds are grateful and repay attention. I wonder where my maid is? Petra! [*Signals for her maid.*]

DON GONZALO. [*Aside, looking at* LAURA, *whose back is turned.*] No, no, I will not reveal myself. I am grotesque now. Better that she recall the gallant horseman who passed daily beneath her window tossing flowers.

DOÑA LAURA. Here she comes.

DON GONZALO. That Juanito! He plays havoc with the nursemaids. [*Looks* R. *and signals with his hand.*]

DOÑA LAURA. [*Aside, looking at* GONZALO, *whose back is turned.*] No, I am too sadly changed. It is better he should remember me as the black-eyed girl tossing flowers as he passed among the roses in the garden. [JUANITO *enters by* R., PETRA *by* L. *She has a bunch of violets in her hand.*]

DOÑA LAURA. Well, Petra! At last!

DON GONZALO. Juanito, you are late.

PETRA. [*To* DOÑA LAURA.] The guard gave me these violets for you, señora.

DOÑA LAURA. How very nice! Thank him for me. They are fragrant. [*As she takes the violets from her maid a few loose ones fall to the ground.*]

DON GONZALO. My dear lady, this has been a great honor and a great pleasure.

DOÑA LAURA. It has also been a pleasure to me.

DON GONZALO. Goodbye until tomorrow.

DOÑA LAURA. Until tomorrow.

DON GONZALO. If it is sunny.

DOÑA LAURA. A sunny morning. Will you go to your bench?

DON GONZALO. No, I will come to this—if you do not object?

DOÑA LAURA. This bench is at your disposal.

DON GONZALO. And I will surely bring the crumbs.

DOÑA LAURA. Tomorrow, then?

DON GONZALO. Tomorrow!

[LAURA *walks away toward* R., *supported by her* MAID. GONZALO, *before leaving with* JUANITO, *trembling and with a great effort, stoops to pick up the violets* LAURA *dropped. Just then* LAURA *turns her head and surprises him picking up the flowers.*]

JUANITO. What are you doing, senor?

DON GONZALO. Juanito, wait——

DOÑA LAURA. [*Aside.*] Yes, it is he!

DON GONZALO. [Aside.] It is she, and no mistake. [DOÑA LAURA *and* DON GONZALO *wave farewell.*]

DOÑA LAURA. "Can it be that this is he?"

DON GONZALO. "Heavens, is it she?" [*They smile once more, as if she were again at the window and he below in the rose garden, and then disappear upon the arms of their servants.*]

CURTAIN

MOZART AND THE GRAY STEWARD

by

THORNTON WILDER

The popular belief that the dying Mozart was ordered to write his own death-music or requiem has persisted through the years. This poetic dramatization of the legend invents a ghostly character in the form of a steward.

Thornton Wilder's one-acters stem from his early period when as a young man he planned a series of sketches to be called *Three Minute Plays for Three Persons*. Since then he has written other one-act plays. Among these are *The Trumpet Shall Sound, The Long Christmas Dinner,* and *The Happy Holiday*. The longer plays which have made him famous are *Our Town*, which won the Pulitzer Prize in 1938, and *The Skin of Our Teeth* written in 1942.

Mr. Wilder has always regarded himself as first, a teacher, and secondly, a writer.

THORNTON WILDER
BEST KNOWN FOR "OUR TOWN."

MOZART AND THE GRAY STEWARD

CHARACTERS

CONSTANZE

MOZART

THE GRAY STEWARD

MOZART *is seated at a table in a mean room in Vienna or-chestrating the "Magic Flute." Leaves of ruled paper are strewn about the floor. His wife enters in great excitement.*

CONSTANZE. There's someone come to see you, someone important. Pray God, it's a commission from Court.

MOZART. [*Unmoved.*] Not while Salieri's[1] alive.

CONSTANZE. Put on your slippers, dear. It's some one dressed all in gray, with a gray mask over his eyes, and he's come in a great coach with its coat of arms all covered up with gray cloth. Pray God, it's a commission from Court for a *Te Deum* or something.

[*She tidies up the room in six gestures.*]

MOZART. Not while Salieri's alive.

CONSTANZE. But, now, do be nice, 'Gangl, please. We must have some money, my treasure. Just listen to him and say "yes" and "thank you" and then you and I'll talk it over after he's gone.

[*She holds his coat.*]

Come, put this on. Step into your slippers.

MOZART. [*Sighing.*] I'm not well. I'm at home. I'm at work. There's not a single visitor in the whole world that could interest me. Bring him in.

---

[1] An Italian composer of operas, unfriendly to Mozart, while he lived in Vienna.

CONSTANZE. [*Adjusting his stock.*] Now don't be proud. Just accept.

[*She hurries out and presently reenters preceding the visitor. The visitor is dressed from head to foot in gray silk. His bright eyes look out through the holes in a narrow gray silk mask. He holds to his nose a gray perfumed handkerchief. One would say: an elegant undertaker.*]

THE GRAY STEWARD. Kappelmeister Mozart, *servus*. Gracious lady, *servus*.

MOZART. *Servus*.

THE GRAY STEWARD. Revered and noble master, wherever music reigns, wherever genius is valued, the name of Wolfgang Amadeus Mozart is . . .

MOZART. Sir, I have always been confused by compliments and beg you to spare me that mortification by proceeding at once to the cause of your visit . . . the . . . the honor of your visit.

THE GRAY STEWARD. Revered master, before I lay my business before you, may I receive your promise that—whether you accept my commission or not—you both will . . .

MOZART. I promise you our secrecy, unless our silence would prove dishonorable to me or injurious to some one else. Pray continue.

THE GRAY STEWARD. Know then, gracious and revered genius, that I come from a prince who combines all the qualities of birth, station, generosity and wisdom.

MOZART. Ha! a European secret.

THE GRAY STEWARD. His Excellency moreover has just sustained a bitter misfortune. He has lately lost his wife and consort, a lady who was the admiration of her court and the sole light of her bereaved husband's life. Therefore, his Excellency, my master, commissions you to compose a Requiem Mass in honor of this lady. He asks you to pour into it the height of your invention and that wealth of melody and harmony that have made you the glory of our era. And for this music he asks leave to pay you the sum of four hundred crowns,—two hundred now, and the second two hundred crowns when you deliver the first four numbers.

MOZART. Well, Constanze, I must not be proud.

THE GRAY STEWARD. There is but one proviso.

MOZART. Yes, I heard it. The work must represent the height of my invention.

THE GRAY STEWARD. That was an easy assumption, master. The proviso is this: You shall let his Excellency have this music as an anonymous work, and you shall never by any sign, by so much as the nod of your head, acknowledge that the work is yours.

MOZART. And his Excellency is not aware that the pages I may compose at the height of my invention may be their own sufficient signature?

THE GRAY STEWARD. That may be. Naturally my master will see to it that no other composer will ever be able to claim the work as his.

MOZART. Quick, give me your paper and I will sign it. Leave your two hundred crowns with my wife at the foot of the stairs. Come back in August and you will have the first four numbers. *Servus. Servus.*

THE GRAY STEWARD. [*Backing out.*] *Servus,* master. *Servus,* madame.

[CONSTANZE *returns in a moment and looks anxiously towards her husband.*]

CONSTANZE. A visit from Heaven, 'Gangl. Now you can go into the country. Now you can drink all the Bohemian water in the world.

MOZART. [*Bitterly.*] Good. And just at a time when I was contemplating a Requiem Mass. But for *myself.* However, I must not be proud.

CONSTANZE. [*Trying to divert him.*] Who can these people be? Try and think.

MOZART. Oh, there's no mystery about it. It's the Count von Walsegg. He composes himself. But for the most part he buys string quartets from us; he erases the signatures and has them played in his castle. The courtiers flatter him and pretend that they have guessed him to be the composer. He does not deny it. He tries to appear confused. And now he has succeeded in composing a Requiem. But that will reduce my pride.

CONSTANZE. You know he will only be laughed at. The music will speak for itself. Heaven wanted to give us four hundred crowns—

MOZART. And Heaven went about it humorously.

CONSTANZE. What was his wife like?

MOZART. Her impudences smelt to Heaven. She dressed like a page and called herself Cherubin. Her red cheeks and her black teeth and her sixty years are in my mind now.

CONSTANZE. [*After a pause.*] We'll give back the money. You can write the music, without writing it for them.

MOZART. No, I like this game. I like it for its very falseness. What does it matter who signs such music or to whom it is addressed?

[*He flings himself upon the sofa and turns his face to the wall.*]

For whom de we write music?—for musicians? Salieri!— for patrons? Von Walsegg!—for the public? The Countess von Walsegg! I shall write this Requiem, but it shall be for myself, since I am dying.

CONSTANZE. My beloved, don't talk so! Go to sleep.

[*She spreads a shawl over his body.*]

How can you say such things? Imagine even thinking such a thing! You will live many years and write countless beautiful pages. We will return the money and refuse the commission. Then the matter will be closed. Now go to sleep, my treasure.

[*She goes out, quietly closing the door behind her.* MOZART, *at the mercy of his youth, his illness and his genius, is shaken by a violent fit of weeping. The sobs gradually subside and he falls asleep. In his dream* THE GRAY STEWARD *returns.*]

THE GRAY STEWARD. Mozart! Turn and look at me. You know who I am.

MOZART. [*Not turning.*] You are the steward of the Count von Walsegg. Go tell him to write his own music. I will not stain my pen to celebrate his lady, so let the foul bury the foul.

THE GRAY STEWARD. Lie then against the wall, and learn that it is Death itself that commissions. . . .

MOZART. Death is not so fastidious. Death carries no perfumed handkerchief.

THE GRAY STEWARD. Lie then against the wall. Know first that all the combinations of circumstance can suffer two interpretations, the apparent and the real.

MOZART. Then speak, sycophant, I know the apparent one. What other reading can this humiliation bear?

THE GRAY STEWARD. It is Death itself that commands you this Requiem. You are to give a voice to all those millions sleeping, who have no one but you to speak for them. There lie the captains and the thieves, the queens and the drudges, while the evening of their earthly remembrance shuts in,

and from that great field rises an eternal *miserere nobis*.
Only through the intercession of great love, and of great art
which is love, can that despairing cry be eased. Was that
not sufficient cause for this commission to be anonymous?

MOZART. [*Drops trembling on one knee beside the couch.*]
Forgive me.

THE GRAY STEWARD. And it was for this that the pretext
and mover was chosen from among the weakest and vainest
of humans. Death has her now, and all her folly has passed
into the dignity and grandeur of her state. Where is your
pride now? Here are her slippers and her trinkets. Press
them against your lips. Again! Again! Know henceforth
that only he who has kissed the leper can enter the kindom
of art.

MOZART. I have sinned, yet grant me one thing. Grant
that I may live to finish the Requiem.

THE GRAY STEWARD. No! No!

[*And it remains unfinished.*]

Questions and Topics for Discussion

TWO SLAPS IN THE FACE

Questions

1. Should Vilma have laughed?
2. Would any other girl have acted as Vilma did?
3. What does Alfred mean by chivalry?
4. Is Vilma's conduct easy to explain?
5. Can reason be applied to this problem?
6. Why is it hard for teen-age boys to understand teen-age girls?

Topics for Discussion

The ups and downs of teen-age love.
Logic and love: do they go together?

PROLOGUE TO GLORY

Questions

1. Why did so many die of milk-sick?
2. Explain: "We grow in love and arrive at grace abounding."
3. What are young Lincoln's views of slavery?
4. What two sorrows in life afflicted Lincoln?
5. Explain Abe's final line.
6. Does the final line recall a line from "Macbeth?"

Topics

Lincoln Legends

LINCOLN PLAYS YOU WILL ENJOY:

Lawyer Lincoln by CHASE WEBB and BETTY SMITH
The Boy, Abe by BETTY SMITH
Abe Lincoln in Illinois by ROBERT SHERWOOD
Shirt Tail Boy by W. P. COVINGTON III

TOO MANY HANDS ON A WATCH

Questions

1. Why was the missing watch valuable?
2. How does the author create anxiety over the missing watch?
3. Is Tillie's suspicion sensible?

243

4. Why is Mr. Fossel's pride hurt?
5. Is it right to reward robbery?
6. Is it true that to an expert, all suckers are easy?
7. Express in a phrase the underlying idea of the play.

Topics

The Adventures of a Watch
Cheating a Cheater
Sleight-of-Hand Tricks

FINGER OF GOD

Questions

1. How does Strickland give himself away?
2. Was the girl's choice of the name, Alfred Stevens, accidental?
3. Why is Strickland's conduct criminal?
4. Is the girl's confidence justified?
5. Does Strickland's confession come naturally?
6. How is Strickland's wild streak tamed?
7. Is the final decision forced?
8. Does thinking oneself honest lead to honesty?
9. Where do you find the Finger of God moving?

Topics

The Troubles of Honesty
"I'm going to face the music."
Last-minute confessions in life (in plays).

THE OWL AND TWO YOUNG MEN

Questions

1. What's wrong with Jim and Jerry?
2. Is the coincidence sad or funny?
3. What books have the boys been reading?
4. How does the girl's entrance change everything?
5. How does the owl fit into the scene?
6. Explain the joke in "the revival of the fittinest."
7. In what part of the country is this dialect spoken?

Topics

Odd Expressions
Puppy Love
Teen-age Triangles

LOVE IN THE APE HOUSE

Questions

1. What makes the setting unusual?
2. Are Herbert's suspicions valid?
3. What is Florrie's problem?
4. Does the ape help Florrie?
5. Does Florrie love Herbert?
6. Do you admire Florrie's quick wit?
7. With which character do you sympathize?

Topics

Career vs. Heart
Plays on the Theme of Jealousy.
Dramatizing Situations in Life

IN THE ZONE

Questions

1. Why do so many plays take place in a forecastle or fo'c's'l?
2. How are the different nationalities projected?
3. Which details add up to suspicion?
4. Are the reasons for suspicion easy to forgive?
5. Do you admire Jack?
6. Why do we sympathize with Smitty?
7. What secret of Smitty comes to light?
8. How is the situation at the end saved?

Topics

Traveling in Danger Zones
Seamen at Sea
Personal Secrets Bared in Public

MATERIA MEDICA

Questions

1. What are the duties of a probationer nurse?
2. Explain the words: pharmacology, therapeutics, materia medica.
3. Why can't Marguerite concentrate?
4. How do experienced nurses look upon their job?
5. What did a doctor say to Marguerite?

6. How does Marguerite betray her feelings?
7. Are we prepared for the final scene?

Topics

Popular Notions about Nurses
Hospital Humor
Slips of the Tongue

THE UGLIEST MAN IN THE WORLD

Questions

1. What is meant by the stream-of-consciousness method?
2. Trace the slow build-up of Paul Martin's ugliness.
3. How does each episode add to Martin's torture?
4. Why is the reading from "Cyrano" fitting?
5. Do you feel the love of the blind girl is true?
6. In the final quotation, what is meant by "that sudden sun?"
7. Show that physical ugliness may be overcome by spiritual or inner beauty.

Some Technical Terms Explained

fade—diminish volume
up—increase the volume
down—decrease the volume
filter—thin down the voice: change the tone quality
echo chamber—a space through which sound is channeled to give sounds a far-away quality

QUARE MEDICINE

Questions

1. What line in the beginning expresses Henry's character?
2. Is Mattie a typical wife?
3. How does the father fit into the scene?
4. Is there humor in the line, "Lay the law down, Henry."
5. Is Dr. Immanuel an ordinary medicine-faker?
6. Is the doctor's soliloquy good theatre?
7. Name the steps in the cure of Henry.
8. What is the men's idea of freedom?
9. Is there humor or pathos in the plot?

Topics

Courage by Suggestion.
Henpecked Husbands
Medicine-fakers, Mountebanks, and Pitchmen.

RED DEATH

Questions

1. Trace on a map the region known as the Southland.
2. Describe the mark of death.
3. Why is the date, 1915, important?
4. How many ways are there of saying Red Death?
5. Should the doctors have laughed at Dr. Goldberger?
6. Did Dr. Goldberger prove his theory?

Topics

Heroes of Science
The Dangers of Experiment
Serving Your Fellow-men

ENTER THE HERO

Questions

1. What is meant by "the romantic attitude?"
2. Explain: "Girls are funny things, aren't they?"
3. When Harold arrives, how does Anne act?
4. Show how the dream differs from the actual.
5. Is Anne the victim of the tragic attitude?
6. Point out a few comic moments.
7. Is Harold right to feel enraged? Explain.
8. How do you explain Anne's romantic streak?
9. With whom do you sympathize: Anne or Harold?
10. Will Anne change?

Topics

The Pleasure of Self-deception
Is Make-Belief all Fun?
When Fact Meets Dream

A SUNNY MORNING

Questions

1. Prove that the opening lines are an "ill-natured prelude?"
2. How do the old man and the old lady differ?
3. What do you learn of their early lives?
4. Do the "aside" remarks help or hinder?
5. Why does each one pretend the affair happened to another?
6. Why does each refuse to admit his identity?
7. With what feeling did the play leave you?

Topics

Castles in Spain
Romance Never Dies
Romance Among the Aged

MOZART AND THE GRAY STEWARD

Questions

1. Show how Death is made to represent the age of Mozart.
2. Who was Salieri?
3. Why must the Requiem be anonymous?
4. Is the dream device effective?
5. Does the Gray Steward make a pleasant impression?
6. What is the point of the closing line?

Topics

Compare the presence of Death in this play with one from any other.

RECOMMENDATIONS

To Write A Playlet

The Technique of the One-Act Play B. ROLAND LEWIS
The Craftsmanship of the One-Act Play PERCIVAL WILDE
Writing the One-Act Play HAROLD N. HILLEBRAND
How to Write a Play ROBERT FINCH

To Direct A Play

Amateur Theatre Handbook EUGENE DAVIS
Drama Clubs Step by Step CHARLES F. WELLS
The Play Produced JOHN FERNALD
Producing a Play ROBIN STARK
Stage Craft for Amateurs F. A. MARTEAU and JOHN HOLGATE
A Primer of Stagecraft HENNING NELMS
Stagecraft Manual E. T. STUMP and R. E. HOLCOMBE
Play Production MILTON SMITH
The Stage in Action SAMUEL SELDEN
The Art of Play Production JOHN DOLMAN, JR.

To Act

Acting: The First Six Lessons RICHARD BOLESLAVSKY
The Actor Creates ARISTIDE D'ANGELO
An Actor Prepares CONSTANTINE STANISLAVSKI
Actors on Acting COLE, TOBY, and CHINOY
The Act of Acting JOHN DOLMAN
Drama in Schools and Youth Centers G. H. HOLROYD and NORA RATCLIFF
Face the Footlights E. B. COLVAN
First Steps in Acting SAMUEL SELDEN
Rehearsal MIRIAM A. FRANKLIN
Modern Acting ROSENSTEIN, HAYDON, SPARROW

To Read Playlets

CERF, BENNETT and CARTMELL, VAN H. EDS. *Thirty Famous One-Act Plays*
CLARK, B. H. ED. *Representative One-Act Plays by British and American Authors*

CLARK, B. H. and COOK, T. R. EDS. *One-Act Plays*

CLARK, B. H. and NICHOLSON, K. EDS. *The American Scene*

CLEMENTS, C. C. ED. *Sea Plays*

COHEN, H. L. ED. *One-Act Plays by Modern Authors*

EASTMAN, FRED ED. *Plays of American Life*

ELIOT, SAMUEL A. J. ED. *Little Theatre Classics*, 4 Vols.

FINCH, ROBERT ED. *Plays of the American West*

GARRIGUS, FRED ED. *You're On the Air* (radio)

GRIFFITH, F. J. and MERSAND J. EDS. *One-Act Plays for Today*

HOLROYD, GEORGE H. ED. *Miniature Dramas* 4 vols.

HUGHES, GLENN ED. *Short Plays for Modern Players*

ISAACS, EDITH J. R. ED. *Plays of American Life and Fantasy*

JOHNSON, THEODORE ED. *Miniature Plays for Stage and Study*

JOHNSON, THEODORE ED. *Still Another Book of Miniature Plays*

JOHNSON, THEODORE ED. *Plays in Miniature*

JOHNSON, THEODORE ED. *Ten International One-Act Plays*

KOZLENKO, WILLIAM ED. *Twenty-five Non-Royalty One-Act American Comedies*

KOZLENKO, WILLIAM ED. *One Hundred Non-Royalty One-Act Plays*

KOCH, FREDERICK H. ED. *Carolina Folk-Plays*, 3 series

KOCH, FREDERICK H. ED. *Carolina Folk Comedies*

LEONARD, STERLING A. ED. *The Atlantic Book of Modern Plays*

LEWIS, B. R. ED. *Contemporary One-Act Plays*

LOCKE, A. LeR and GREGORY, M. EDS. *Plays of Negro Life*

MARTIN, CONSTANCE M. ED. *Fifty One-Act Plays*

MAYORGA, MARGARET ED. *Representative One-Act Plays by American Authors*

MAYORGA, MARGARET ED. *Twenty Short Plays on a Royalty Holiday* I, II

MAYORGA, MARGARET ED. *Plays of Democracy*

MOSES, MONTROSE J. ED. *Representative One-Act Plays by Continental Authors*

NICHOLSON, K. ED. *Appleton's Book of Short Plays*

PORTMANTEAU PLAYS

PROVINCETOWN PLAYS

RICHARDSON, WILLIS AND MILLER, MAY EDS. *Negro History in Thirteen Plays*

SHAY, FRANK ED. *Contemporary One-Act Plays* (American)

SHAY, FRANK ED. *Fifty Contemporary One-Act Plays*

SHORT PLAYS FOR MODERN PLAYERS

SMITH, A. M. ED. *Short Plays by Representative Authors*

SMITH, BETTY ED. *Twenty-five Non-Royalty One-Act Plays for All-Girl Casts*

SMITH, BETTY ED. *Twenty Prize-Winning Non-Royalty One-Act Plays*

SMITH, M. M. ED. *Short Plays of Various Types*

TEN ONE-ACT PLAYS

THOMAS, CHARLES S. ED. *The Atlantic Book of Junior Plays*

TOTHEROH, DAN. *One-Act Plays for Everyone*

TUCKER, S. M. ED. *Twelve One-Act Plays for Study and Production*

TUCKER, S. M. ED. *Plays for Amateurs: A Selected List*

WEBBER, J. P. AND WEBSTER, H. H. EDS. *One-Act Plays for Secondary Schools*

WILDE, PERCIVAL *Three-Minute Plays*

Annual Series

One-Act Plays for Stage and Study
Famous Plays of 1932-33 . . . Continued
Best One-Act Plays edited by MARGARET MAYORGA
One-Act Plays of Today edited by J. W. MARRIOTT
Yearbook of Short Plays edited by WISE AND SNOOK

Radio Plays

BARNOUW, ERIK *Radio Drama in Action*

BOYD, J. ED. *The Free Company Presents*

CORWIN, NORMAN *More*
    Pursuit of Happiness
    Thirteen
    Twenty Six
    We Hold These Truths
    Words Without Music
    This Is War

CUTHBERT, MARGARET *Adventure in Radio*

LAWTON, S. P. *Radio Drama—Radio Continuity Types*

LISS, JOSEPH *Radio's Best Plays*

MACLEISH, ARCHIBALD *The American Story*: 10 Broadcasts

MORRIS, JAMES *Radio Workshop Plays*

OBOLER, ARCH *Fourteen Radio Plays*
          Ivory Tower and Other Radio Plays
          Oboler Omnibus
          Plays for Americans
          This Freedom
          To the President
ROLO, CHARLES J. *Radio Goes to War*

PROMINENT WRITERS OF ONE-ACT PLAYS
Suitable for Study Units

JOHN K. BANGS	GLENN HUGHES
J. M. BARRIE	W.W. JACOBS
SYDNEY BOX	ALFRED KREYMBORG
ALICE BROWN	MARY MACMILLAN
HAROLD BRIGHOUSE	PERCY MACKAYE
GEORGE CALDERON	MAURICE MAETERLINCK
E. P. CONKLE	ALBERT MALTZ
NOEL COWARD	GEORGE MIDDLETON
HAROLD CHAPIN	EDNA ST. V. MILLAY
BEULAH M. DIX	CLIFFORD ODETS
THEODORE DREISER	EUGENE O'NEILL
LORD DUNSANY	DAVID PINSKI
FRED EASTMAN	LYNN RIGGS
RACHEL FIELD	WELDON STONE
JOHN GALSWORTHY	AUGUST STRINDBERG
ALICE GERSTENBERG	ALFRED SUTRO
SUSAN GLASPELL	J. M. SYNGE
KENNETH S. GOODMAN	RIDGELY TORRENCE
PAUL GREEN	STUART WALKER
LADY GREGORY	PERCIVAL WILDE
LAURENCE HOUSMAN	THORNTON WILDER
WM. D. HOWELLS	TENNESSEE WILLIAMS

WM. BUTLER YEATS